DEAF STUDENTS IN
LOCAL PUBLIC HIGH SCHOOLS

DEAF STUDENTS IN LOCAL PUBLIC HIGH SCHOOLS
Backgrounds, Experiences, and Outcomes

By

THOMAS N. KLUWIN, PH.D.
Gallaudet University

MICHAEL S. STINSON, PH.D.
National Technical Institute for the Deaf

CHARLES C THOMAS • PUBLISHER
Springfield • Illinois • U.S.A.

Published and Distributed Throughout the World by
CHARLES C THOMAS • PUBLISHER
2600 South First Street
Springfield, Illinois 62794-9265

This book is protected by copyright. No part of
it may be reproduced in any manner without
written permission from the publisher.

© *1993 by* CHARLES C THOMAS • PUBLISHER
ISBN 0-398-05865-2
Library of Congress Catalog Card Number: 93-16870

With **THOMAS BOOKS** *careful attention is given to all details of manufacturing and design. It is the Publisher's desire to present books that are satisfactory as to their physical qualities and artistic possibilities and appropriate for their particular use.* **THOMAS BOOKS** *will be true to those laws of quality that assure a good name and good will.*

Printed in the United States of America
SC-R-3

Library of Congress Cataloging-in-Publication Data

Kluwin, Thomas N.
    Deaf students in local public high schools : backgrounds,
experiences, and outcomes / by Thomas N. Kluwin, Michael S. Stinson.
      p.   cm.
    Includes bibliographical references and index.
    ISBN 0-398-05865-2
    1. Deaf—Education (Secondary)—United States—Case studies.
2. Mainstreaming in education—United States—Case studies.
I. Stinson, Michael S.   II. Title.
HV2545.K58   1993
362.4′2′071173—dc20   93-16870
                                                                                CIP

To
Bridget and Susan
and
Angela, Greg, and Emily

ACKNOWLEDGMENTS

The longitudinal study of deaf adolescents in local public schools was not the result of the efforts of a single individual but of many people across the country who contributed to make this project possible. The contributions of all of those who have helped in this endeavor need to be recognized.

To begin with, there has been a steady stream of talent who passed through Gallaudet University and helped maintain the records of this work. These include Mary Simpson, Elena Jiminez Ulloa, Lucy Trivelli, Kate Tobin, Catherine Sweet, and Arlene B. Kelly.

There has been a faithful group of individuals in different locations around the United States who have helped collect and send us much of the data that is reported in this book: Ann Levis, Jim Newman, Milt Graves, Pam Balkovec, June Kempf, the late Jane Landis, Wendy Gonsher, Susan Steege, Mary Ann Ziegler, Mary Lou Casey, Charles Osler, Connie Smith, Tracie Daley, Pat Robertson, Elizabeth Royal, Carrie Perez, Ardalia Idelbird, Cheryl Moses, Harriet Kaberline, Sheila Barnard, Carolyn Rowland, Hartley Koch, Barbara MacNeil and Candy Schauer. Without their assistance, this book would not have been completed.

The co-investigators for this project in addition to the authors were Martha Gonter Gaustad of Bowling Green State University; Lynne Blennerhasset and James Woodward of Gallaudet University; Suzanne King of the Douglas Hospital Research Centre; and Kathleen Whitmire of Syracuse University. While the authors are responsible for the contents of this specific book, portions of the data set are the efforts of those named above. These individuals suggested and modified existing instruments or developed entirely new instruments that were used as part of this study. We would also like to acknowledge the support of the Gallaudet Research Institute in general and Donald F. Moores of the Center for Studies in Education and Human Development in particular for their support of the longitudinal study.

CONTENTS

Chapter   *Page*

1. Responding to Changes in Deaf Education   3
2. The Background of Our Study   17
3. Where Do They Come From?   33
4. Courseloads, Programs, and Tracking   53
5. Interacting with Peers   73
6. Participation in Extracurricular Activities   87
7. Development of Social Competence   109
8. Achievement and Grade Point Average   123
9. Getting a Perspective   137

Bibliography   153
Index   161

DEAF STUDENTS IN
LOCAL PUBLIC HIGH SCHOOLS

Chapter 1

RESPONDING TO CHANGES IN DEAF EDUCATION

Recently, patterns of educational placement for deaf children have undergone significant changes. Over the past two decades, there has been a trend toward educating deaf children in public schools on a commuting basis as a result of post-World War II demographic changes, changes in the structure of American cities accompanied by changes in the transportation system, and the impact of the 1964–65 rubella epidemic on the deaf population. As a result, now more than 70% of deaf children are educated in local public school programs (Schildroth, 1988). This is readily contrasted with the situation at the end of the Second World War when there were three discrete sub-systems: public residential schools for the deaf, public day schools for the deaf, and private residential schools for the deaf (Moores, 1992). The patterns of school placement for the deaf, influenced by a number of demographic variables, have become much more complex since World War II. While deaf children still attend residential schools, significant numbers of programs for the deaf in local public schools have been established.

Much is made of PL 94-142 and its impact on deaf education; however, as seen in the figures reported by Moores (1992) much of the castigation of PL 94-142 within deaf education obscures a much longer running trend in the education of deaf children in the United States. Essentially, residential school populations—according to Moores' figures—reached their maximum in about 1910 followed by a steady state situation. During the Great Depression, the numbers of deaf students in residential schools rose because of an influx of hard of hearing youngsters from large families that saw an opportunity for better care for their children. Nonetheless, the maximum number of available educational spaces was achieved in about 1910 (Moores, 1992).

Following the end of World War II, residential school populations began a steady decline which was buoyed slightly by an increase in the number of deaf children due to the overall increase in the general population. However, this trend began to run out by the early 1960's as the "Baby Boom" ended. A rubella epidemic in 1965 created a twenty year counter trend in deaf education. While the general school population started a steady decline, the number of deafened individuals increased dramatically within a single year. This population bulge rapidly overran the resources of the state residential school systems and by the late sixties public school programs, experiencing a decline in their populations, were beginning to take up the excess population, particularly the less severely hearing impaired.

The rubella epidemic along with changes in attitudes towards manual communication during the late sixties and early seventies as well as profound changes in child rearing practices as "Baby Boomers" began to reproduce contributed as much to the decline of residential schools and the rise of local public school programs as much as any specific legislation.

As manual communication—generally referred to as "Total Communication"—was reintroduced into residential school programs, it also began to make inroads into local public school programs when it became apparent that through the use of interpreters, deaf children who before would have been problematic as far as a mainstream placement was concerned could now be placed in a regular classroom with an interpreter. A little later in the decade, a profound social change occurred—best represented by the appearance of Linda Bove as a regular cast member on "Sesame Street." Profoundly deaf adults without intelligible speech were beginning to be seen as contributing members of a diverse society. A generation of hearing children were being raised with the notion that deaf adults who signed were as normal as Gordon, Maria, Mister Hooper, or Big Bird, and that signing was an acceptable mode of communication.

As "Baby Boomers" began to reproduce, they drastically changed American sexual and reproductive mores. Often the products of large families, American women of that generation began to limit the number of their offspring to one or two children and to delay both marriage and childbirth from several years to a decade or more in some social strata. The result was tremendous pressure for the "perfect child" as seen in a rise in litigation against obstetricians for real and perceived malpractice during birth. Since these women had delayed child bearing, were limiting the number of children in their families, and often were sacrificing satisfying careers for child raising, pressure was building to keep handicapped children at home.

PL 94-142 enters the picture in 1974 as a legal, not a social landmark, in the education of the deaf. Essentially, it provided the formal basis for a movement already underway. The change in deaf education was from the dominance of residential schools over a system that at one time included large numbers of local day schools to a mixed system of special schools including residential schools and local public schools (Moores, 1992). Given that only one quarter of deaf children are in state residential schools and half of them commute on a daily basis, the current topology of the field would suggest a three way division among special schools, large county-wide or multi-district programs for the deaf, and tiny programs primarily for pre-schoolers (Kluwin, 1992a).

A RESEARCH BASED RESPONSE TO CHANGE

Three issues arose during the early 1980's that motivated the study described in this book: the continued de-institutionalization of special education students and particularly deaf students, a renewed demand for excellence in American public education, and a renewed concern for high school as a critical transition period between childhood and adulthood. Above, we discussed the process of the shift from residential schools to local public schools. Now, we need to turn to a brief discussion of the other two forces that were at work in American education at the start of this research project.

Throughout the history of the United States, the history of education has been bound up with the notion of the perfectibility of its citizenry. The first public education established in Massachusetts in the seventeenth century saw the goal of perfectibility in the desire to aid citizens to avoid evil. By 1983, Boyer (p. 301) would proclaim that, "Without excellence in education, the promise of America cannot be fulfilled." As this project comes to press, the skill, ability, and productivity of the American worker is again the benchmark for the measure of educational quality as it was one hundred years ago. However, when this project began, the work of Boyer (1983) had just come out and preliminary reports from Coleman's work (Coleman & Hoffer, 1987) were just appearing in the professional and public press. In the early 1980's, the social turmoil of the seventies was behind a nation newly confident but concerned nonetheless over its ability to maintain its position in the world. A series of educational studies had highlighted the apparent decline in American educational standards during the previous decade. Consequently, a new call went out for excellence in education.

At the same time, the local public school education of deaf children had arisen. Deaf education was simultaneously confronted by two problems. First, the field knew virtually nothing about the operation of local public school programs; and second, the field was placing deaf students in an unknown territory that appeared to be in considerable trouble. As deaf education within the context of local public school education headed for a troubled and unknown future, there was a need to respond to the call for increasing the quality of local public school education. In response to this massive and largely undocumented change in the process of deaf education, we conducted a five year longitudinal study of 451 deaf students as they moved through public high school programs in 15 different cities or counties around the United States.

MEET SOME EXAMPLES OF
DEAF STUDENTS IN LOCAL PUBLIC SCHOOLS

In the process of collecting and analyzing the data from this project, we encountered several general types of students. The terms "deaf" or "hearing impaired" or "mainstreamed" are inadequate to describe the diversity of the children we found or the complexity of their individual experiences.

There was John, a young man with a moderate hearing loss and a reading level beyond high school when he started ninth grade. John maintained a high cumulative grade point average throughout high school, was in mainstream settings without an interpreter, and his primary mode of communication in school was speech. All of his friends were hearing since he had virtually no contact with the deaf education program. The youngest in his family with affluent, married, and well-educated parents, John primarily used speech at home.

Also, there was Jim, another white male on grade level in reading at the start of ninth grade, who used speech during his elementary school years. While most of his friends were hearing, a major difference between Jim and John was that Jim's hearing loss was severe. A notable difference between the families was that in Jim's house there were some telecommunication devices for the deaf such as a TDD for the phone and a caption decoder for the television.

Among the many minority group students we saw was Latoya, a profoundly deaf, black female who was reading at the sixth grade level at the start of ninth grade. Her elementary school experience included special classes and non-academic mainstreaming. Her preferred mode of communication was signs. She had both deaf and hearing friends because since starting high school she had been mainstreamed into math classes and had some extracurricular experience with hearing peers. Latoya was the oldest child in her family. Her parents were married, well educated, and comfortably well-off. The primary mode of communication with Latoya at home was speech. Her parents expected Latoya to complete college and most likely become a teacher. They were interested in her progress in school and had shown some adjustment to her deafness in that they owned both a TDD and a television decoder.

Chrissy was a white female, with a severe hearing loss, who read at the fourth grade level at the start of high school. Chrissy was primarily in mainstream settings in elementary school but experienced a variety of communication situations. Because she had contact with both deaf education and general education programs, she had friends in both settings; however, her preferred mode of communication was speech with both groups. Her parents, who had high school educations and were still married, primarily used speech at home. Her parents had conflicting expectations for her, that is, they expected her to achieve only average grades and complete only vocational training after high school; but they would have liked her to have a job that required a college education.

Another young man was Carlos, an hispanic who read at the third grade level at the start of high school. He had some academic mainstreaming during his elementary school years. His preferred mode of communication in high school was sign language with both his deaf and hearing friends. During elementary school, he experienced a number of different communication philosophies. Carlos's family had no contact with the school program he was in.

Molly, a white female who read below the third grade level at the start of high school, had a profound hearing loss and was in special classes throughout elementary school where her primary mode of communication was varied but included sign language. All of Molly's friends were deaf and came from the school program. Like Carlos, Molly's family was not involved with the school program.

As we can see from these vignettes, the students in public school programs for the deaf vary on the basis of race, gender, hearing loss, ability, and family resources. In addition, the children experience different communication philosophies, friendship patterns, and placement situations. These various factors influence the early education of the child as well as the child's subsequent school achievement. In this book we will describe how we tracked the progress of a national sample of deaf students like the six we just described as they moved through American public high schools.

A RANGE OF PROGRAMS AND AVAILABLE SERVICES

Because public school programs are, for the most part, of relatively recent vintage, they do not have the structural stability of the state residential schools. Consequently, public school programs for the deaf cannot be readily categorized. We observed five different types of programs during our study:

1. mildly impaired, higher achieving affluent students in scattered sites (1 program);
2. severely impaired, moderately achieving, primarily white students in central suburban sites (3 programs);
3. lower achieving minority students in central urban sites (5 programs);
4. centrally sited, county-wide programs with a diverse population who fall around the average for degree of hearing loss and achievement (3 programs).
5. Anomalous programs included:
    a. a very small, regional day school,
    b. a city-wide program in the same city as the state residential program, and
    c. a city-wide program with a diverse population.

The first type described is not anomalous because while it does not share traits with the other programs in our study, there are other types of programs with the same dispersion of locations and organizational structure outside of our data base, particularly in Pennsylvania and New York state.

Affluent, Suburban Programs with Scattered Sites

While this may be a common model (Kluwin, 1992a), only one program in our study fit into this category. Because of the difficulties of data collection when students are scattered over a large geographic area, we purposely avoided working with programs like this. It was felt at the outset of the project that such programs would produce serious communication and logistics problems over the years.

The program we worked with, East 1, was an administrative unit for the suburban districts surrounding a large, metropolitan area. The function of the program was to coordinate services to single students or small groups of students in local schools, usually in a resource room configuration. This program served over 300 students with a staff of 28 which included 26 teachers, an administrator, and a secretary.

Ethnically and economically, this program was quite unique. It had minority staff members but no minority group students. Serving the suburbs of a large city, its population was entirely white but covered the full range of economic categories while maternal education matched the overall economic picture. The hearing loss of its students reflected its fundamental organization; that is, students with generally less severe hearing losses dispersed across several sites.

Suburban Programs at a Central Site

For the most part, these programs served "bedroom" communities near large metropolitan areas. In general, students were from more affluent, white families.

Northeast 2 was a county-wide program accountable to the local school district and housed by grade level and communication philosophy at specific sites; however, both the oral and the total communication programs operated at the same high school site. In this study, only the secondary school service unit was involved. This included a student body of about 70 with 26 staff members. Nearly one-half of the staff were teachers while the rest included a single administrator, a secretary and an interpreting team.

Suburban, central site programs shared many similar traits such as ethnic distribution, family resources, and achievement levels in the ninth grade; however, they were in very separate geographic areas.

Midwest 2 was an administrative unit for the suburban districts surrounding a large metropolitan area. The secondary school program for the deaf was housed at a single high school. Midwest 2 was the high school site for a larger "umbrella" organization like East 1. Unlike East 1 which was organized on a resource room model, Midwest 2 was more of a regional day school model in that it housed a large number of deaf students at one site with a mix of special classes and mainstreamed settings.

California 1 was a middle school/secondary school program which drew from several elementary school districts among the suburbs of one of the larger California metropolitan areas. Middle school and junior high students were housed at one site while the high school students were at another site. The program was operated by the county department of education to serve grades six through twelve at the two campuses. The staff included teachers of the deaf, educational aides, educational interpreters, a transcriber, a psychologist, a counselor, audiologists, speech therapists, career specialists, and a part time nurse. The two sites each had a mainstream resource teacher who provided educational support for deaf students and who consulted every two weeks with the regular classroom teacher. Students participated in all extra-curriculars with full interpreting services. In addition there was a chapter of the Junior National Association of the Deaf (NAD). A specific work program was not offered but career education was included in various academic subjects. In addition, students' vocational interests were evaluated by a career specialist. Students in their junior and senior years could participate in either occupational programs or work experience. The administrator of the deaf education program functioned as a "principal" within the building with responsibility for the deaf education program. Most students were white and very affluent, reflecting the position of the county as one of the wealthiest in the nation.

Centralized Urban Programs

Urban, minority, and lower achieving characterize centralized, urban programs. While the ethnic distribution within each program was unique, there was a common thread of a larger percentage of non-white students than the national average.

Northeast 1 was one of the oldest urban programs for the education of the deaf in the United States. It consisted of two sites. The primary site combined a K–6 hearing program and a K–12 self-contained program for the deaf. During junior and senior high school, those students who were to be mainstreamed were sent to a local junior or senior high school where Northeast 1 operated a program on a resource room model with interpreters for the students.

The high school program offered instruction in special classes to about 45 adolescents. Both middle and high school students had two periods daily in a vocational class taught by a teacher of the deaf. In addition three to five students each year attended a half day vocational training course at the city-wide occupational reserve center with an interpreter-tutor. A satellite secondary school program was operated in a local high school for about ten students supported by two teachers of the deaf and two interpreter tutors. The high school program had a strong work/study program that offered students work placements in local business and industry. Nine out of ten graduates of the central site program were placed in competitive jobs at graduation. Support services for the students at the central site included a social worker, speech and language therapist, psychologist, diagnostic teacher of the deaf, and an audiologist. Other services included a Spanish interpreter/liaison/tutor.

Northeast 3 was a large urban program with the secondary level total communication site housed at one high school with hearing students. Over 500 hearing impaired students were served by the city-wide program which had a total staff of 78. At the high school site, the program was developing throughout the course of our study and was managed by an itinerant school psychologist and counselor. By the end of the study, the school psychologist-counselor had become a permanent fixture as program director in the building. The program included separate classes for the deaf as well as a small interpreting team to support the mainstreamed students. Deaf students rode public transportation from considerable distances to reach the school site.

California 2 was a division of a city public school system with students placed at site schools on the basis of communication mode and grade level. During the course of this study, this program experienced considerable re-organization due to across the board school age population reductions and shrinking funding. At the start of the study the preschool to grade 12 program served nearly 300 deaf and hard of hearing students and included a specialist for the deaf as its head with several full-time deaf education specialists. By the end of the study, there were no deaf education specialists without classroom assignments and the director was also responsible for several other non-deafness related handicaps. At the classroom level, the double-track, or oral program at one site and the total communication program at another site, by a grade levels model was still in place (Kluwin, 1992a). The program employed counselors and school psychologists on a program-wide basis with a special emphasis on hiring deaf professionals.

Centrally Sited, County-Wide Programs

The achievement of the students in centrally sited, county-wide programs is in the middle of the distribution for all of the programs in our study; but these programs enjoy another trait in common as well. They are county wide programs which draw from a diverse ethnic group.

Average hearing loss for these programs falls around the grand mean for the entire sample.

Southeast 1 was a division of one of the largest public school systems in the United States (128,000 students). Special facilities had been built on the sites of two elementary, one middle and one high school. In addition, itinerant instruction was provided to some students in their neighborhood schools. System-wide staff included a curriculum supervisor, a program monitor, three audiologists, speech clinicians, certified teachers of the deaf, interpreters, a preschool psychologist, and special counselors for deaf students.

Southeast 2 was a division of a county-wide public school system. The overall program served about 200 students from pre-school to grade 12 at specific sites organized by grade level. Reflecting the broad age range, only 40% of the staff of 42 were teachers. The rest of the staff included parent-infant specialists, audiologists, and some interpreters for the mainstreamed students. It is a characteristic of programs that serve younger deaf populations that a larger percentage of the staff are not teachers (Kluwin, 1992a).

Texas 1 was a regional program for the deaf which included the urban and suburban districts of one of the larger Texas metropolitan areas. Preschool and infant services were provided under contract to a local university center while elementary, junior high school, and senior high school programs were based at specific sites. The staff for the entire K–12 program included teachers of the deaf, aides and aide/interpreters, supervisory teachers, and various support staff.

The program was administered through the local school district which housed the office of the director of the regional day school program. The director reported directly to the school district's director of special education.

The local public school district served 125,000 children while the program for the deaf served an additional 22 neighboring school districts. The secondary school program was housed at a comprehensive high school of 1,550 students in grades nine through twelve. The day to day functioning of the program for the deaf was the responsibility of the supervisor of the high school program. This individual functioned as an assistant principal within the school building. Interpreting was handled by a professional interpreting staff certified by the school district using a system based on RID certification standards. Interpreters were used in classrooms, assemblies, and for extra-curricular activities. The high school program had a part-time counselor. A vocational adjustment counselor divided her time between the deaf education program and the multi-handicapped program.

Texas 2 was a regional program for the deaf which included the urban and suburban districts of one of the larger Texas metropolitan areas. Preschool and infant services were provided while elementary, junior high school, and senior high school programs were based at specific sites. Staffing included a director, two supervisors, a high school counselor, a parent-infant facilitator, speech therapists, vocational adjustment coordinator, a work evaluator, teachers of the deaf and interpreter/aides. At the elementary level there was a parent-infant program that included weekly visits by the coordinator with a Spanish language interpreter as needed. At the middle school campus, the school was under the building administrators as far as everyday situations were concerned. Students' vocational skills were evaluated in eighth grade. When the students graduated to ninth grade, these evaluations were used as the basis for four year vocational plans for each student. The high school program was directly responsible to the building administrator with the deaf education specialists functioning as consultants. The program traditionally included an active vocational evaluation and work experience program at the secondary level.

Texas 3 was a regional program for the deaf which included the urban and suburban districts of one of the larger Texas metropolitan areas. Infant and preschool services were provided. Elementary age deaf students were housed at a school for exceptional children while junior high school and senior high school students were housed at conventional schools.

Anomalous Programs

South 1 was a regional day program for the deaf administered by a city school district with all of its students at the school site. Mainstreaming was accomplished by sending the students to local high schools. There were several levels of mainstreaming. Some students were mainstreamed in local schools and were provided itinerant services via the regional program while others were mainstreamed at a local high school with support services as needed. In addition, there were special classes for the deaf at the day school site. Other services included an adaptive physical educator, an audiologist, several instructional aides, interpreters, an occupational therapist, two speech pathologists, a vocational educator, and a full-time registered nurse. South 1, while being a central site regional program, also served a small and less severely impaired population.

Texas 4 was a regional program for the deaf. This was a small program, less than one hundred students from pre-school to grade 12, because of its proximity to the state residential school for the deaf.

Midwest 1 was a day school model for a local city-wide public school program. The overall program served about 250 students from pre-school through high school at a central site. Of the total staff of 68, 59 were teachers. Support staff included audiologists and counselors.

A FRAMEWORK FOR DISCUSSION

We began this work in nearly total ignorance of how public school programs for the deaf operated on a day-to-day basis. Consequently, it would be less than honest of us to present an elaborate "a posteriori" theoretical framework for this project. However, we did begin the project with some general concerns, and more importantly we began it with some very specific limitations: a low incidence handicap, a desire for a study that was national in scope, and the vagaries of funding support for a longitudinal study. Nonetheless, the early direction for the project was guided to a large extent by the work of Herbert Walberg (1984) on effective schools as well as a serious concern for producing a project that was responsive to the operation of the schools themselves (Kluwin, 1991).

While the project did not completely conform to the detail's of Walberg's model of school effectiveness, we sought to remain as much as possible within many of the areas of concern that he had defined. The resulting collection of information was a compromise between our interests, some serious theoretical concerns, and the limits imposed on us by limited and uncertain funding.

The simplest possible organizing device for the quantity of information that we collected would be chronological. Within this framework, we collected information on basically five areas of concern: invariant traits, pre-high school experiences, ninth grade traits, high school experiences, and high school outcomes.

By invariant traits, we mean those characteristics of youngsters over which schools have no control such as gender, race, family, socioeconomic status, (Walberg, 1984) and in the case of deaf children, the degree of their hearing impairment (Wolk *et al.*, 1982). Pre-high school experi-

Figure 1.1
Overall Analysis Plan

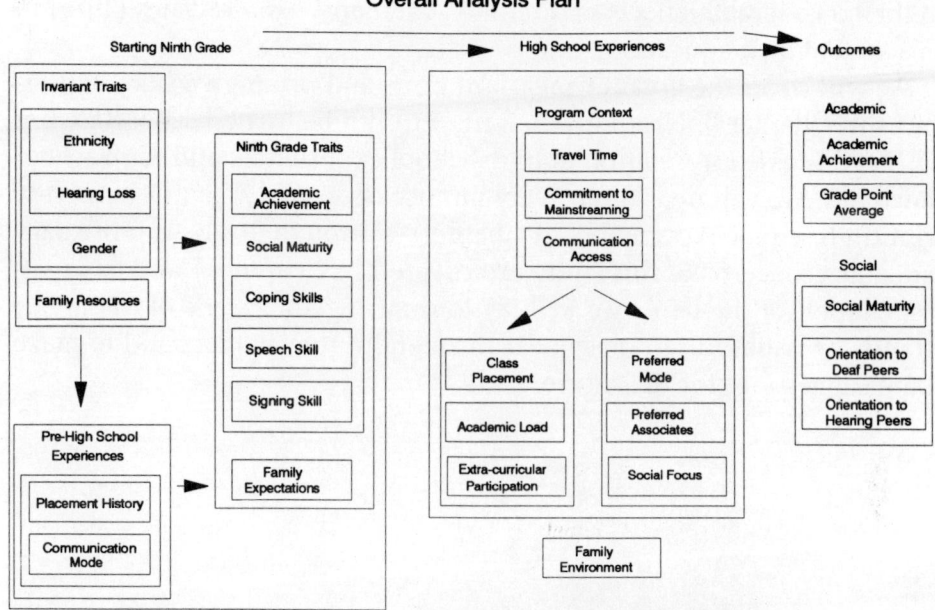

ences covers the child's education experiences prior to ninth grade and includes such issues as the age of entry into schooling, type of communication philosophy used in grade school, and degree of transience during the grade school years. Ninth grade traits refers to those school related abilities that a child has as she or he enters high school including reading level, mathematics ability, and social or emotional maturity. High school experiences includes academic and non-academic experiences. Academic experiences includes the types and number of courses a student takes. In the case of deaf adolescents, it also includes the placement of the child, that is, was the child in a mainstream class, a resource room, or a self-contained class? Non-academic experiences includes participation in sports and extra-curriculars as well as the student's contact with his or her peers. School outcomes is essentially an arbitrary category which reflects the value system of those studying American schools. Our interests at the outset covered three areas; academic achievement, social integration, and the capacity to enter adulthood. Obviously, academic achievement is an established American educational goal. For deaf students, social integration into hearing society, deaf society, or both is a critical issue. Unfortunately, we did not clearly define the concept of transition to adulthood at the start of the project; consequently, we will have to remain moot on that outcome. The interested reader is referred to the considerable efforts of Thomas Allen and his associates (1989) in this area of deaf education.

We will cover the areas of invariant traits and pre-high school experiences in Chapter 3. Ninth grade traits will not be treated separately but will be discussed in relation to high school experiences and high school outcomes. We will deal extensively but not necessarily comprehensively with high school experiences in Chapters 4 through 6. The two primary outcomes concerns of this study are covered in Chapters 7 and 8. In the last chapter of the book, we will try to draw together some of the major strands or issues raised piecemeal throughout the chapters and to make some suggestions for the future.

Chapter 2

THE BACKGROUND OF OUR STUDY

The first organizational meeting for the project took place from July 1 through July 3, 1986. Representatives of eight large public school programs for the deaf were brought to Gallaudet University in Washington, D.C. to discuss issues that they considered critical to the future of public school programs for the deaf.

The scope of the project, presented at this meeting, was to be a four-year longitudinal study of the achievement, social integration, and career aspirations of deaf adolescents in public school programs. The goals of the study were:

1. to provide descriptive data on these programs and the students in them,
2. to answer specific issues about the most appropriate types of programming for deaf adolescents,
3. and to generate usable educational innovations through a process of continuous interaction with operating school programs.

The operating principles of the study were to be relevant to the needs of the schools, to be as unobtrusive as possible in the daily functioning of the schools, and to provide as rapid and as meaningful information as possible to school personnel (Kluwin, 1991).

The original design called for 200 students from 5 school districts to participate in the study.

Due to a very positive response from the University administration to the initial group and to the goals of the project, a second group of seven individuals representing six additional public school programs was brought to Gallaudet University several months later in the hope of expanding the scope of the project. Consequently, the potential data base was expanded to include an estimated 400 deaf students who were currently in ninth and tenth grades.

The following year, the research team assembled to discuss the future direction of the longitudinal study and to develop plans for collaborative projects. The primary focus of the meeting was on the "social—emotional component" of the study since until that point the focus of the study had been measures of achievement. Shortly after this, the administrators of the programs met with the research team to discuss the new direction and the additional data collection. At this point 15 schools had become involved in the longitudinal study. One of the results of the successful first year was an agreement by the administrators of the programs to include the then current ninth grade class in the project.

Table 2.1
DATA COLLECTION PLAN

SCHOOL YEAR	86–87	87–88	88–89	89–90	90–91
GRADUATING CLASS	89,90	89,90,91			
GRADE LEVEL	9,10	9,10,11			
ARCHIVAL INFORMATION					
Annual Survey Data	X, X				
SAT–HI Scores	X, X			X	X
Enrollment History	X, X				
Course Reports	X, X	X, X, X	X, X	X	
GENERAL INFORMATION					
Writing Sample	X, X		X	X	
Meadow-Kendall	X, X		X	X	
SPECIFIC PROJECTS OR INFORMATION					
Family Demographics		X, X, X			
Student Communication		X, X, X			
ACOPE		X, X, X			
Social Activity Scale			X, X, X	X	X

Based on this revised data collection plan the number of subjects rose to over 450. The number of subjects in the study varies from citation to citation in this report for several reasons. First, as is apparent from the preceding narrative, the project expanded in two major jumps, that is, from seven to 15 schools and from two cohorts to three. Second, as will be described in detail in Chapter 3, subjects dropped in and out of the project quite readily. Our best estimate is that about 9% of the names we had in the study at any given time were not "real," that is, they entered and exited their programs within a single year or less or they came to us by accident. A third reason is that entire programs would periodically "drop out" or become non-responsive usually as the result of a change in administrators.

Subsequent years of the project followed generally the same pattern.

The year started with a meeting with the school administrators to review the previous year's progress, to outline future activities, and to get input from the administrators in regard to work that might be done. Following this meeting, an annual data collection plan was sent out and followed. During each year, attempts were made to collect data not collected during the previous year with major efforts launched each year as a group got ready to graduate. Along the way some specific interventions were developed as a service activity for the schools to encourage their continued cooperation (see Kluwin, 1991, Kluwin & Kelly, 1990).

Given the fact that the half-life of a public school administrator is about four years and we worked with 15 programs at the start of the project, each year involved a considerable degree of "fence mending." Contact people died, changed jobs voluntarily, were fired, or retired. Each year, we lost contact for part of the time with between one fourth and one half of the programs. Table 2.1 above provided a summary of the data collected. The following discussion expands on Table 2.1 in detail.

PROCEDURES

Instrumentation

Annual Survey Data.

Through the permission of the parents of the children in the study and with the cooperation of the schools and the Center for Assessment and Demographic Studies, background information on the students was obtained through the Annual Survey of Hearing Impaired Children and Youth. This information included the date of birth, sex, race, degree of hearing loss, etiology, and onset of deafness for each subject in the longitudinal study. Where this information was not available from the Annual Survey, forms were sent to the schools in order to obtain comparable data from school records.

Stanford Achievement Test Hearing Impaired Version.

This is a widely used test for assessing the academic achievement of deaf children. This test is one of the better achievement tests available and gives a reasonably good estimate of performance. Consequently, this data was generally available in school records and would be collected on a regular basis by the schools. In the case of schools that did not, other arrangements were made.

The subtests used were the reading comprehension, the mathematics concepts, and the mathematics computation subtests.

Enrollment History.

A form was sent to the schools in order to document the previous educational history of the subjects in the longitudinal study. Information was requested about the name of the child's school, the mode of communication used, and the type of placement of the child from preschool through eighth grade. Mode of communication was coded as oral, total communication, cued speech, other, or unknown. Placement types included separate classes for the deaf, mainstreamed for non-academic classes, mainstreamed with an interpreter for some academic classes, mainstreamed with an interpreter for all academic classes, mainstreamed without an interpreter, in some or all academic classes, resource room support, and unknown.

Course Reports.

In June of each year the schools were asked to provide information on the students' progress in school. The requested information included the subjects taken, the type of placement, any changes that might have occurred during the year, and the final grade received. A follow-up for missing data was conducted in the spring of 1990 and again in the fall of 1991.

Placement types were defined as separate class for the deaf, mainstreamed with an interpreter on a daily basis, mainstreamed with periodic interpreting, mainstreamed without an interpreter, access to resource room, and unknown. A table was developed to equate courses by titles across the different schools.

Writing Evaluation.

The 13 year-old stimuli from the National Assessment of Educational Progress were used (Kluwin & Kelly, 1990). The descriptive essay, the persuasive letter, and the business letter were administered to the oldest cohort in the tenth grade and to the two younger cohorts in the ninth grade. Students still in the study in twelfth grade were re-tested using the same three stimuli.

Several different scoring systems were used. For the persuasive and descriptive essays, counts were made of the number of words, the number of sentences, the number of clauses, both grammatical and ungrammatical and the number of t-units, or major clauses and subordinated clauses within a sentence.

The descriptive essays were also coded using a six point holistic scoring system. The persuasive letters were coded using a primary trait rating system. Eight points were used in the system ranging from barely comprehensible papers to papers that took a position, provided reasons for the position, developed the points of the argument in detail, and were well organized.

The business letters represented a distinct type of writing from the persuasive and descriptive papers, so a different type of scoring system was used. Because of variations in missing information in the business letter, an individual feature analysis system was used which counted the presence or absence of specific pieces of information such as the greeting, the internal address or the closing. In addition, there were specific content requirements for effective communication about the topic.

In the case of all of the holistic or primary trait rating systems, the same general scoring procedure was followed. During scoring, the two readers discussed the scoring system, the criteria and the anchor papers. Then 20 papers were practiced scored in groups of five to develop reliability.

During the scoring session, each reader assigned a score to a paper. If the two scores were within 1 point of each other, they were accepted as in agreement. The score for the paper was the sum of the scores given by the two readers. In the event of a disagreement, the paper was discussed and the discrepancy was resolved in order to re-establish reliability. When the readers were consistent with each other and the criteria, they then scored blocks of 20 papers each in order to check consistency.

For the holistic scores for the descriptive essays, the readers usually did not differ by more than one point on any paper after training. Consequently, discrepant scores occurred less than 3% of the time. For the persuasive letters, there was a greater tendency for disagreement which was largely related to the variability in the responses of the writers to the stimulus. On the average, about 10% of each set of persuasive essay scores were not in agreement.

As was said above, five types of information were counted on the descriptive essays and on the persuasive essays in order to generate a measure of grammatical complexity: total words, total sentences defined orthographically, total t-units, total grammatically correct clauses, and total semantic clauses. From these counts, three measures of syntactic complexity were computed: words per clause, words per t-unit, and clauses per t-unit for both the descriptive essay and for the persuasive essay.

To generate trait scores for the business letter, the scores for the categories were added together to form two traits: form and content. Form consisted of positive ratings for the use of an internal address, correct date, appropriate greeting and closing. Content consisted of use of the correct full name, a return address, a reference to the item, a request for the item to be sent, a specification of which item to send, and the absence of extraneous information.

To develop factor scores for the writing test, the holistic score for the descriptive essay, the primary trait score for the persuasive essay, the business form score, the business content score, and three measures of syntactic complexity were factor analyzed. The three measures of syntactic complexity were the number of words per grammatically correct clauses, the number of grammatical correct clauses per t-unit, and the percentage of grammatically correct clauses. This factor analysis yielded two factor scores: rhetorical skill and syntactic complexity.

Table 2.2
FACTOR SCORES FOR THE WRITING TESTS
Factor Loadings
(n = 422)

Measure	Rhetorical Skill	Syntactic Complexity
Clauses/t-unit	.156	.860
Words/clause	.231	.857
Correct clauses	.171	.913
Persuasive Trait	.742	.383
Descriptive Holistic	.778	.246
Business Form	.816	.077
Business Content	.806	.102

Meadow-Kendall Social Emotional Inventories.

Two copies of the Meadow-Kendall Social Emotional Inventory were sent to the schools for each of the youngsters in the study at the start of the project and again when the students were in twelfth grade. The schools were asked to select the two teachers who were most familiar with the students and to have them fill out the forms. Teachers were paid five dollars for each completed form to compensate them for their time and effort.

There are two major types of reliability to be addressed in considering the Meadow-Kendall: internal consistency and rater reliability. To test the internal consistency of the scale, three Cronbach's alphas were computed: Social Adjustment = .949; Self Image = .906; Emotional Adjustment = .812.

Because over 90 different individuals rated the students, it was not practical to compute a rater reliability figure, consequently, to adjust for rater differences, the mean of the two ratings from the same time period was used as the best approximation of the true rating.

ACOPE.

Pilot Study. Prior to the large scale testing, two pilot tests, where the students read the test with help if they requested it, were conducted on 38 students at two locations in California. It was noted with these deaf adolescents that less able readers had considerable difficulty with some of the language on some of the items. Consequently, a signed version of the inventory was developed in order to reduce possible reading effects.

Main Study. Printed copies of the ACOPE and a copy of the videotape stimulus for the ACOPE were sent with a cover letter and return envelopes to each of the school systems. The instrument was presented to the students in print and on videotape simultaneously (Kluwin, Blennerhasset, & Sweet, 1990). A skilled signer presented the items of the inventory in Pidgin Sign English without voice to compensate for less able readers. A practice page was presented to the subjects before giving them the actual inventory.

Subjects were tested in small groups in their classrooms. A person familiar with the subjects passed out the practice pages, explained that it was a practice, and went through the practice page with the students. The individual items on the practice page were signed to the students by the test administrator.

The actual inventories were then distributed to the subjects. The purpose and directions for the test were explained to the students by the test administrator using manual communication. The videotape was controlled so that students had time between the signing of each item in order to respond to the item. If a student had a problem, the tape was stopped, and the item was explained without hinting at a specific answer.

Subscale scores were computed based on the original factors generated by the authors of the scale. Subscale reliabilities ranged from .706 to .325 for the original subscales.

Validity. In an attempt to establish construct validity for the ACOPE, the subscales of the ACOPE were correlated with the three subscales of the ninth grade administration of the Meadow-Kendall. Because so many statistics were computed, the significance level was set at .01 to avoid spurious correlations. None of the correlations were statistically significant.

Given the generally poor reliability and concurrent validity for the twelve original ACOPE scales for what is a large and fairly representative sample of deaf adolescents, it was decided to generate a more stable set of scores. A factor analysis produced three new scales with alpha coefficients of .809, .615, and .704 respectively.

Table 2.3
NEW FACTOR SCORES FOR ACOPE

Positive actions include:
Obey parents; Apologize; Talk to teacher; Go shopping; Talk to parents; Self-improvement; Think good thoughts; Say nice things; Go to church; Organize life; Work hard in school; Try to get close; Help other people; Talk to mom; Do what I enjoy; Make new friends; Wish for better; Talk to sibling; Do something with family; Pray; See good side of situation; Never drink booze; Sleep; Talk to dad; Talk to friend; Strenuous exercise

Destructive actions include:
Cry; Get angry; Complain to friends; Do drugs; Swear; Blame others; Try to get even; Solve by self; Problem not important; Wish better; Smoke; Drink booze; Say mean things; Complain

Avoidance actions include:
Listen music; Eat food; Avoid home; Use prescription drugs; Involved at school; Go shopping; Become involved with boy/girlfriend; Ride in car; Joke; Do drugs; Do what enjoy; Help from others; Make new friends; Go to movie; Work harder; Smoke; Drink booze; Video games

Social Activity Scale.

The purpose of the Social Activity Scale was to provide information on student perceptions of their social relationships in and out of school. It also provided information on identity formation in the sense that part of identity formation is with whom one associates and feels most comfortable with.

Table 2.4
SOCIAL ACTIVITY SCALE
Items for the three dimensions

Participation.
Subscales dealt with participation (a) in the classroom (e.g. "In my mainstream classes, I talk with hearing/hearing-impaired students"), and (b) at school (e.g. "I have lunch with hearing/hearing-impaired friends"). As can be seen, for each type of participation, there were two subscales of corresponding items, with one referring to hearing and the other to hearing-impaired peers. Students responded on 5-point scale indicating frequency of participation: *never, two or three times a year, about once a month, about once a week,* and *everyday*. Additional subscales dealt with participation in out of school social activities (e.g. "Go to parties at hearing/hearing-impaired friend's homes"). For these, students responded on a 4-point scale: *never, once or twice a year, about once a month, about once a week,* and *everyday*.

Relatedness.
Subscales tapped need for closer relationships (e.g. "I wish I had more friends who were hearing/hearing-impaired") and emotional security (e.g., "When I'm with hearing/hearing-impaired students my age, I feel nervous."). Students answered on a 4-point scale: *almost never, not very often, most of the time,* and *always*.

Perceived Social Competence.
One subscale asked about ability and success in establishing good peer relationships (e.g., "I feel nervous in groups of people."). These items did not distinguish between relationships with hearing and hearing-impaired peers. Students responded on a 4-point scale: *not at all true of me, a little true of me, mostly true of me,* and *very true of me*.

For each of these areas, there was a set of questions regarding deaf peers and a parallel set regarding hearing peers. An additional scale asked about perceived social competence.

While these sets of items comprise the Social Activity Scale, the questionnaire also requested additional information. These questions asked about extent of mainstreaming, perceived number of friends and participation in extracurricular activities.

Pilot Study. Prior to the large-scale administration of the Social Activity Scale to students in the study, pilot testing was conducted with 34 students in Ontario and Florida. It was observed that some students had difficulty understanding the wording of several items; consequently these were rephrased to make them more easily understood.

Data Collection. The Social Activity Scale was administered from

February to June during the 1988–89 academic year and was then given to each student as she or he was completing twelfth grade. Two forms of the Social Activity Scale were used: one for students who had at least some mainstream experience during the year and one for students who were always in special classes. The only difference in the two forms was that the one for special placements did not contain four items which asked about interaction with hearing students in mainstream classes. The Social Activity Scale was administered to groups of one to four students by a person familiar with them, such as a teacher or interpreter. Each student received a copy of the questionnaire to complete with pencil. The examiner read aloud or read aloud and signed the directions. The examiner also read to the student as many of the items in the scale as was desirable to ensure maximum comprehension. Thus, for some students the examiner read all the items, but for others, the examiner read none. The examiner indicated on the first page of the questionnaire the extent that questions were read aloud or signed to the student. Students completed four or five practice items to familiarize themselves with the Likert-type scale that they used to answer the subsequent set of items. For example, for the set of questions pertaining to in-class interactions with hearing peers, students responded on a NEVER to EVERYDAY continuum. (The first question was, "In my mainstream classes, I talk with hearing students.")

Family Background Information and FACES.

FACES is a family cohesion questionnaire that, along with an internally developed questionnaire about socioeconomic status, family communication, and family expectations was sent out during the first week of January, 1989. Ninety-five of the parents responded to this first mailing. During mid-March a follow-up mailing was done. A third mailing was done at the end of May. The final response rate was 59%.

In addition to the third mailing, school personnel were queried on some of the family demographic information for those families who did not respond to the questionnaire. This information included marital status, family size, communication mode used in the family, and parents' occupations.

Two scores were initially computed for the FACES inventory: family cohesion and family adaptability. From these two scale scores, types of families were describable. The "balanced" family represents the midpoint in the tension between the two scales of cohesion and adaptability. Extreme families fall away from this central point.

To create a usable cohesion and adaptation index, a score was computed for each dimension which consisted of the absolute value of the difference between the mean for the dimension and the individual score. Thus, the more extreme a family, the higher their score.

Student Communication Questionnaire.

The students responded to a four-page questionnaire concerning their communication patterns with people at home and school. A sample of the question format follows:

Please show how often THESE PEOPLE use these methods AT HOME to communicate WITH YOU. If the person does not live in your home, put an X in the place before the person. Use the following numbers to show how often.

1 Never
2 Some of the Time
3 Most of the Time
4 All of the Time

	Speaks	Signs	Finger Spells	Writes Notes	Home Signs
Lives with me.					
() Mother	()	()	()	()	()

An analysis of the data patterns revealed two potential problems with interpreting the data from the questionnaire. First, students may have misunderstood the Never-to-all-the-time continuum, thinking that this meant how often communication occurs compared to other activities, and second, students may have been confused by the complexity of the instrument and used a code of "1" to indicate that communication occurred in that mode. An example of the first problem is shown in a student's responses of "Some of the Time" to Speaks and Signs, and "No Response" to the other modes of communication. This response is difficult to interpret because it may mean that the mother uses Speech sometimes, Signs at other times, or it may mean that the mother uses Simultaneous Communication sometimes, although communication is a small part of the day's activities. An example of the second problem is shown in the student's response of "Never" to Speaks and "No Response" to the other modes of communication. It seems likely that this student simplified the task by simply marking only the communication modes used by the mother.

In an effort to salvage the data that could be interpreted, the data were recoded into a new category system. The first step in the recoding process was to change all indications of "never" and all missing or blank data to "0" and to recode any instance of the use of a mode as a "1"; thus, if a student misunderstood the frequency scaling but wished to indicate that he or she used that mode with that individual, he or she would still be counted in the analysis. The second step was to look at all instances of the use of different modes by a single individual; for example, the mother, at one time. This generated several communication mode categories including speech only, speech with a secondary mode not including signs, speech with signs, signs without speech, and other modes.

Operational Definitions of Some Variables Used in the Study

Variables used in later chapters will be described in their appropriate chapter. Outcome measures will be discussed within the context of their own chapters.

As we described in Chapter 1, we adapted Walberg's (1984) model of educational productivity. The following section provides expanded operational definitions of these variables.

Pre-Ninth Grade Characteristics.

Invariant traits. These included the ethnicity of the student, the degree of hearing loss, the gender of the student, and family resources. Family resources is a factor score described below in Table 2.6.

Elementary School Educational Experience. Two variables were generated from the enrollment history forms: the child's placement history and the communication mode history of the child. Placement history was defined as special class placement, variable placement between special classes and academic mainstreaming, single class academic mainstreaming, multiple class academic mainstreaming, and unsupported mainstreaming. Communication mode was defined as primarily oral—including cued speech—variable from oral to total communication, and primarily total communication.

Family Variables. The various family factor scores were created from the parent questionnaire and the FACES inventory. Table 2.5 below presents the factor scores and their loadings. Three factors were generated.

Table 2.5
FACTOR SCORES FOR FAMILY MEASURES

Variable	Family Resources	Family Expectations	Family Environment
Mother's education	.723	.097	−.031
Father's education	.708	.253	−.125
Family income	.750	.129	−.147
Education wanted	.184	.696	.083
Education expected	.129	.163	−.054
Career wanted	.032	.880	−.061
Career expected	.147	.857	−.014
Grades expected	.032	.572	.366
Checks homework	−.109	−.016	.827
Owns decoder	.761	.089	.165
Owns VCR	.462	.108	−.038
Owns TDD	.724	−.057	.134
Family cohesion	−.354	−.290	−.529
Family adaptability	.056	.111	−.405

Family resources includes two dimensions: parental education and parental wealth. Parental education is measured by the number of years of schooling the parents had. Parental wealth is measured by the combined family income and the possession of specific objects: VCR, decoder, and TDD. Family expectations consists of the family's expectations for number of years of school completed by the deaf child, the career that the family wants the child to achieve and assumes the child will achieve, and the parents' expectation for the child's overall grade point average. Family environment is a combination of the family's cohesiveness and adaptability.

Ninth Grade Traits.

Academic Achievement. The measure of academic achievement consisted of the ninth grade scores for the SATHI and the writing measures. Both of these are described earlier in the chapter. To derive a single measure of school achievement, the five available measures were factor analyzed.

The measure of grammatical complexity did not load onto this factor; however, the other four measures did. In essence we have a traditional measure of reading, writing, and arithmetic.

Table 2.6
ACHIEVEMENT FACTOR SCORE

Factor	Weight
Composite writing quality	.820
Grammatical complexity	.084
Reading ability	.792
Mathematics computation	.859
Mathematics concepts	.878

Social Maturity and Coping Skills. There were two sources of data for measures of social or emotional maturity at the start of the study: Meadow-Kendall Social Emotional Inventory Scores and the results of the ACOPE. A factor analysis of the Meadow-Kendall subscales and the ACOPE subscales suggested two dimensions: social maturity and coping skill.

Table 2.7
FACTOR SCORES FOR NINTH GRADE SOCIAL-EMOTIONAL MEASURES

Subscale	Social Maturity	Coping Skill
Social Adjustment	.849	−.002
Self Image	.825	−.080
Emotional Adjustment	.559	.319
Positive Strategies	.181	.772
Avoidance Behaviors	−.456	.629

Social Maturity consists of social adjustment, self-image, emotional adjustment, and the non-use of avoidance activities. Coping skills consists of emotional maturity, the use of positive coping strategies and avoidance coping strategies. Destructive coping behavior formed a completely separate factor which may be related to issues such as dropping out, but is not included in the overall analysis.

Communication Skills. Communication skills measures were generated from the student communication questionnaire which asked the students to rate their communication abilities and the enrollment history form. Table 2.8 below presents the factor loadings.

The preferred mode was rated as oral having a high value and various degrees of signing having lower values; consequently, the negative loading for preferred mode on the speech measure means that those who use speech have less interest in using signs. Conversely, those who rate themselves as good signers also prefer the use of sign language.

Table 2.8
FACTOR LOADINGS FOR COMMUNICATION MEASURES

Variables	Speech Skill	Sign Skill
I can speak	.901	−.162
I can understand speech	.900	−.059
I can sign English	.130	.838
I can sign ASL	−.189	.765
My preferred mode is signs	−.320	.652

Chapter 3

WHERE DO THEY COME FROM?

While every story must start some time and end at another time, events in the real world consist of strands reaching backward and forward from any arbitrary point. We have chosen ninth grade as our starting point, knowing that some of what we need to talk about begins before that point. In this chapter, we would like to convey a sense of who was in the study, demonstrate some critical relationships, and begin to pick up some recurrent themes.

FAMILY TRAITS

Families are an integral part of the education of a child. They influence the child's eventual success in school directly through the physical and economic resources of the family, through the overall emotional climate or family environment that is provided, through the communication of the expectations of the parents regarding school achievement and goals in life, and through specific family activities which promote subject matter learning (Kluwin & Gaustad, 1922). In the tradition of research on family resource variables and school achievement, the two most consistent predictors of school achievement have been maternal education and measures of overall family resources (Alexander & Entwistle, 1988, Forehand *et al.*, 1986; Kinard & Reinherz, 1987; Kluwin & Gaustad, 1992; Page and Keith, 1981; Stevenson & Baker, 1987). From this work it is apparent that specific variables such as maternal education, socioeconomic status, and the presence of a second adult in the home are predictors of student achievement while the impact of family resource variables on achievement can be indirect as well through its influence on parental behavior in support of achievement.

Family environment studies are generally difficult to compare because the definitions of family environments have been quite diverse and factors ancillary to the research such as family structure have been predictors of larger amounts of the variance in school achievement than vague measures of "environment." However, in the studies of family environment specific actions by parents such as consistently enforcing rules are predictors of higher achievement in school (Dornbusch et al., 1987; Forehand et al., 1986).

As Seginer (1983) suggests, a discussion of the impact of family expectations is complicated both by difficulties in defining exactly what expectations are and by operationalizing the process through which expectations are communicated. Ultimately, Seginer concludes that it is not just parental expectations, but also parental supportive behavior that influences the achievement of the child in school. This observation is reinforced through recent work by Coleman and Hoffer (1986) who have pointed out along with others (Alexander & Entwistle, 1988; Durkin, 1975) the impact of specific parent behavior which reinforces school learning.

When we turn to a consideration of parents of deaf school age children, two studies give us some perspective on what occurs (Bodner-Johnson, 1986; Kluwin & Gaustad, 1992). Parental achievement supporting behaviors, parental expectations, and family resources predict a considerable amount of the variance in high school achievement by deaf students. Adaptation to deafness and the availability in the home of assistive devices also explains higher achievement levels among deaf adolescents.

A number of interacting family factors account for the success of children in schools. The primary difference between successful hearing children and successful deaf children appears to be primarily in the area of special adaptations to deafness. Parental resources, higher expectations, and specific behaviors which support learning account for school success in both types of families.

Social Class

Social class can mitigate the effects of deafness in at least two ways. First, through access to better health care, more affluent families can reduce the incidence of some etiologies of deafness or can reduce the severity of the condition through more sophisticated or reliable assistive devices. For example, access to maintenance antibiotics or surgery to drain fluids in the middle ear can result in the elimination of mild progressive hearing losses. Pre-natal care can reduce other etiologies of non-genetic deafness once the condition is diagnosed. Further, greater access to services means an increased likelihood of early diagnosis. The second way that social class can influence the effects of deafness is through access to better services or more intense services. In our study, we had several measures of social class: family income, parental education level, race, and home language (Kluwin & Gaustad, 1991).

Income.

One-fifth of the parents reported incomes of less than $10,000 while only 17.5% of the national population falls below that income level. In addition, nearly twice as many of the incomes of the parents in our study fell in the $10,000 to $15,000 range than would be found in the national population (16%). Median family income for the entire sample was in the $20,000 to $30,000 range. White families had the highest median family income ($30,000 to $40,000 range). Median family incomes for black and hispanic families fell around $10,000. This is somewhat misleading in that income for both of these groups was bimodal. About 40% of both groups had median family incomes of about $10,000, but a second mode of about 40% for both groups fell in the $20,000 to $30,000 range with hispanics trailing blacks. It would appear that our study consisted of more affluent white families and consistently poor minority families.

Parent's Education Level.

The average number of years of education for fathers in the sample was 11.6 with a standard deviation of 3.4 years. Mothers had an average of 11.2 years of education with a standard deviation of 2.6 years.

Asian mothers averaged 12.6 years of school while white mothers had an average of 12.3 years of school. Black mothers had an average of 11.1 years of school while hispanic mothers had only 10.3 years of schooling.

Single mothers had only 11.4 years of school as opposed to married mothers who averaged 12.2 years of school. We suspect that asian mothers have a lower average than reported here because of a bimodal distribution within that subpopulation. Some asian mothers did not respond to any inquiries and schools were not able to provide us with any other information. Our suspicion, based on school personnel comments, is that the nonresponsive asian mothers were those who were less well educated.

Race, Ethnicity, and Home Language.

49% of the sample was white; 26.8% black; 17.1% hispanic; and 6.9% asian. No two programs had the same ethnic distribution. Programs varied from one which had no minority students to three programs where

**Figure 3.1
Mother's Educational Level**

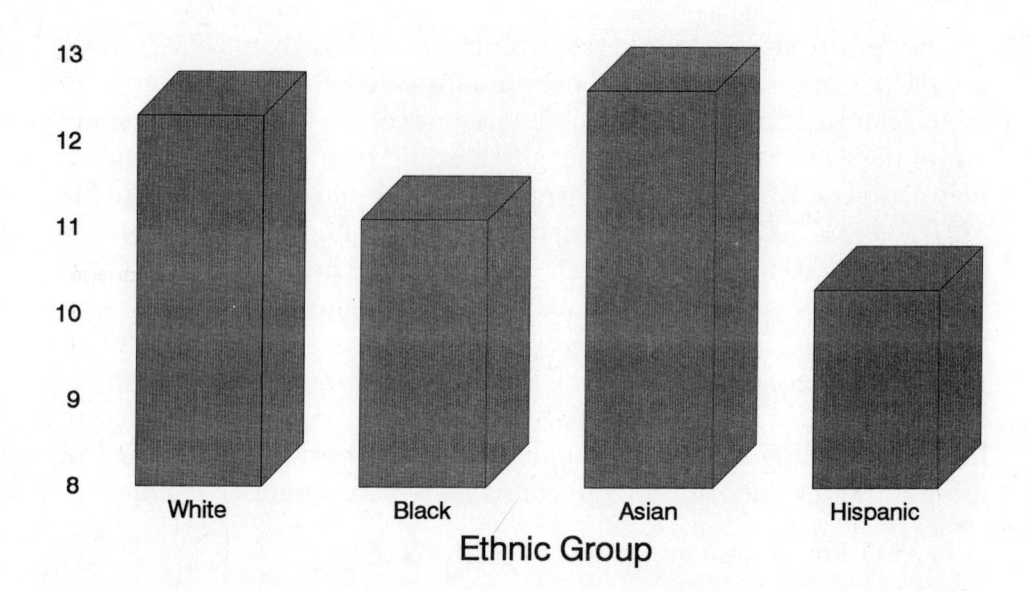

Years in School

[Bar chart showing mother's educational level by ethnic group: White ≈12.5 years, Black ≈11 years, Asian ≈13 years, Hispanic ≈10 years]

Ethnic Group

the majority of students were minorities. There was no program that was predominantly asian, although one California program had a very large percentage of asian students. As would be expected from national demographic trends, programs with predominantly white populations were primarily suburban programs. The programs with large percentages of black students tended to be urban programs. While large hispanic populations were found in traditionally hispanic areas such as Texas or California, a program in the Northeast and one in the Southeast had a large number of hispanic students. There is some anecdotal information from the program staff that the hispanic students in the Northeast, Texas, and California represented three distinct populations. The Texas populations represented a traditional Mexican-American population with a history of hundreds of years in the area. The California hispanic populations were either transients or recent arrivals to the area from Mexico. The hispanics in the Northeast were predominantly from Puerto Rico.

75% of the parents identified English as the primary language used at home. 15% identified Spanish as the primary language spoken at home.

Figure 3.2
Home Language

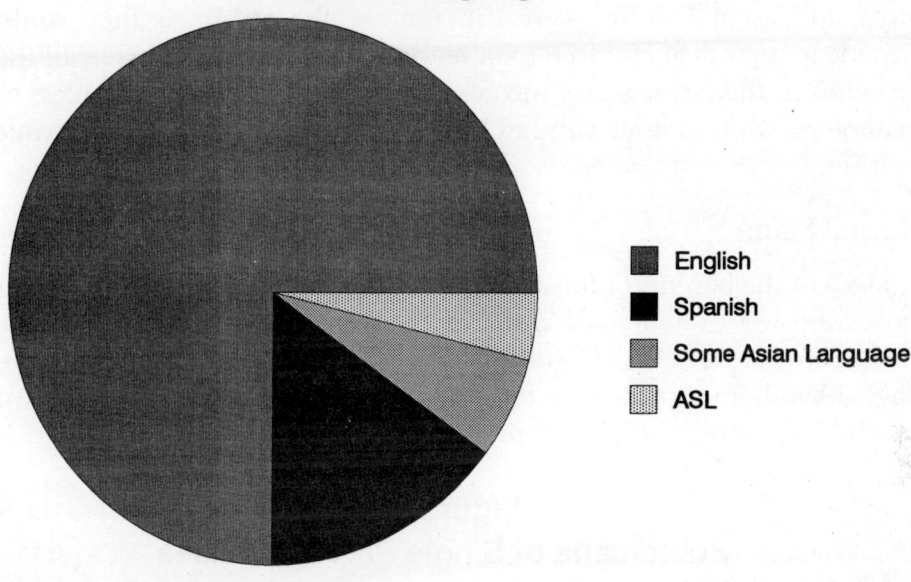

Home Language

- English
- Spanish
- Some Asian Language
- ASL

6% of the sample identified an asian language as the one spoken at home. 4% of the sample said that American sign language (ASL) was the primary language used at home. Our data may underestimate the extent of non-English use in these families because no formal attempt was made to contact non-English speaking families. The project staff relied on the local school programs to interview parents who could not read the questionnaires. This no doubt resulted in some overestimation of English usage; however, the symmetry in the distribution between ethnic identification and language use would argue that the degree of over-estimation of English use may not be too severe.

Family Resources or a Social Class Metric.

In Chapter 2, we described how we generated a family resources variable that represents maternal education, paternal education, family income, and the availability in the home of certain deafness adaptive technology. As a factor score, this variable has a mean of 0 and a standard deviation of .8 for the entire sample. When it is broken down by race, the average score for white families is .37, for asian families .22, for black families −.38, and for hispanic families −.56.

White and asian families had higher family resources scores. A one way analysis of variance (F = 45.33; df = 3,441; p < .001) established that white and asian families were different in the resources they could provide to their deaf children than black or hispanic families. On all the variables in the factor score, income, maternal education, and access to technology, white or asian families lead black families followed by hispanic families.

Marital Status

56.8% of the parents of the students were currently married including those who were remarried. 27.6% of the parents of the children were divorced or separated. 9.6% of the parents were widowed and 6% were single. Another way to look at the situation would be to say that 43.2% of the children were in single parent households.

Figure 3.3
Percentage of Single Parent Families

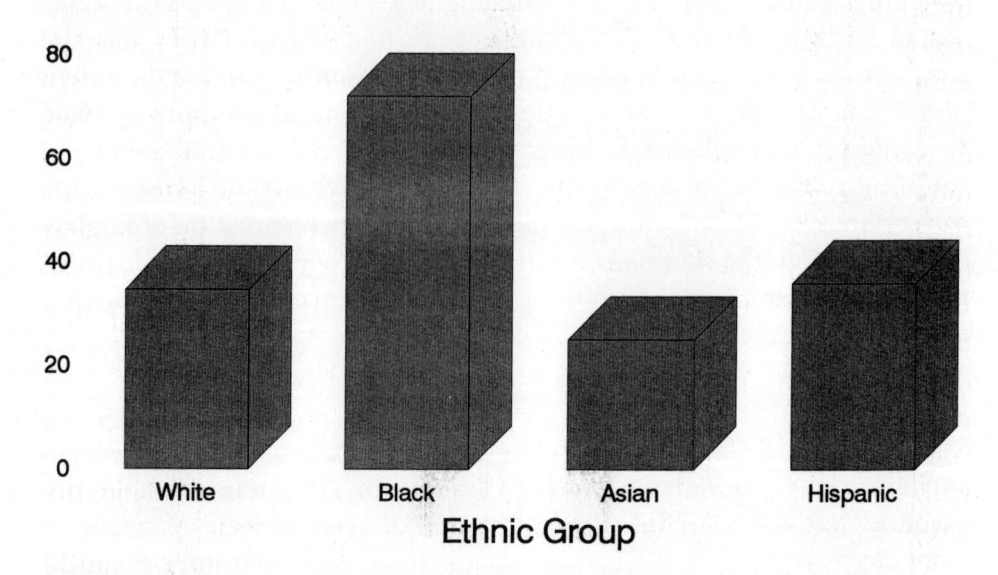

25% of the asian students, 34.6% of the white students, 35.9% of the hispanic students, and 72% of the black students were in single parent households. Median family income for couples was in the $30,000 to

$40,000 range while median family income for single parent households was in the $10,000 to $20,000 range.

Communication Practices

It is important to consider how these families communicated with their deaf children for in the absence of a shared communication system there can be a general sense of isolation of family members (Kluwin & Gaustad, 1991). An apparent negative impact on sibling relationships occurs when hearing siblings turn outward for relationships because they are unable to communicate with a deaf sibling (Luterman, 1987). Another deleterious outcome occurs when mothers may adopt the role of "interpreter" for the child as one alternative to developing a shared communication system within the family (Luterman, 1987).

Kluwin and Gaustad (1991) report that for the mother, the largest single influence on her mode of communication is the child's degree of hearing loss, however, both the child's preschool mode and the mother's degree of education contribute significantly to the mother's use of manual communication with her deaf child. With a greater degree of hearing loss, the use of manual communication in preschool, and a higher level of maternal education, the mother is more likely to use manual communication with the child. For the father, the greatest influence on his mode of communication with the child is the mother's mode of communication followed by the degree of the child's hearing loss and the mode of communication used in preschool. For the siblings, the mother's mode of communication and the deaf child's degree of hearing loss are the most substantial predictors of their mode of communication with their deaf sibling. In conjunction with the level of maternal education and the child's pre-school communication mode, the degree of the child's impairment remains a major consideration in a mother's selection of a mode of communication; and, consequently, a substantial influence on the rest of the family's use of a specific mode of communication. The mother remains the primary decision-maker for the family mode of communication. Influenced by her own educational sophistication, she will base her decision on the child's degree of impairment and the nature of the available services.

Kluwin and Gaustad (1991) have described over 20 different family structure and communication mode situations on the basis of a simple categorization of family members and mode of communication. Earlier, Moores, Kluwin and Mertens (1985) had described 176 unique patterns of communication situations for 185 families. If the simplest approach is taken to the description of family communication practices, three groups tend to fall out: families where all speak to the deaf child, families where all sign in some way to the child, and families that use combinations of methods or have special structures, e.g. single parents without other children. In our data, there is a tendency to symmetry in the communication of mothers of deaf children with their children. 42% of the mothers and children used speech with each other while 48% of the dyads used manual communication. Communication between fathers and the children is not as symmetrical as it is between mothers and the children. Nearly half of the father-child dyads involved speech being used by both parties. In 38% of the dyads, both used some form of manual communication. While less than 1% of mother-child interactions involved forms of communication other than speech or sign, nearly 7% of all father-child dyads involved the use of other modes of communication such as writing notes or simple gestures. Further, due to the prevalence of single parent households, only 76% of the children who reported communication modes used with mothers reported a communication mode with the father.

Family Expectations

As described above, family expectations consisted of the family's desire for a career type for the child, attitude toward what kinds of grades the child should be getting, and the educational attainment level of the child. The factor score had a mean of 0 and a standard deviation of 1. The standard deviation of all of the ethnic groups in our study was also 1 or nearly 1 which suggests that the range of family values is extensive within ethnic groups. On the average, asian parents had the highest expectations for their deaf child (.23) followed by white parents (.06) followed by hispanic parents (−.005) and by black parents (−.02).

The reasonableness of family expectations for their child can be measured in a simple way by comparing the child's standing in relation to other students on the basis of the child's ninth grade achievement and the degree of the parent's expectations for that child. Since both variables are factor scores with a mean of 0 and a standard deviation of about 1, there are essentially identical metrics. By crossing these two metrics we can evaluate the reasonableness of the parent's expectations on a scale from unreasonably low to unreasonably high. For example, a child whose achievement in ninth grade is in the lowest third of the entire sample but whose parents' expectations for the child to succeed are in the top third of the sample would be unreasonably high. When considered this way, nearly half of the parents' expectations were congruent with their child's abilities. 8.9% of the parents had expectations that were unreasonably low for their child and 6.7% of the parents had unreasonably high expectations for their child. The remaining parents were either slightly high or slightly low in the congruence of their expectations and the child's abilities.

Although the asian parents were a small portion of the sample and are thus difficult to discuss because of small cell sizes, they appeared to be generally very accurate in the match of their expectations with the child's abilities. White parents tended to undervalue the child's ability in that they were likely to expect far less from average ability students and not expect enough from very able students. Black parents tended to have greater expectations for less able children while being quite congruent in their expectations for more able children. Hispanic parents tended to be congruent in their expectations in regard to less able students but had unreasonably high expectations for average ability students.

Gender did not appear to be a factor in parental expectations except at the extremes of incongruence; that is, parents of girls were more likely to have unreasonably high expectations and parents of boys were more likely to have unreasonably low expectations. Hearing loss appeared to have a roughly linear relationship with expectations in the sense that parents of less severely impaired students were more likely to have lower than reasonable expectations while parents of more severely impaired students tended to have higher than reasonable expectations. Because of the variation across categories, these were not statistically significant relationships.

The relationship between family resources and the reasonableness of the relationship between the child's ability and the family's expectations was statistically significant ($F = 4.08$, $p < .0$, $df = 4,188$). More affluent and better educated parents were more likely to expect too little of their child while less affluent or well educated parents were more likely to expect more from their child than was reasonable. Others (Seginer, 1983) have interpreted this kind of result to mean that lower social class parents have unreasonable expectations for their child. Our analysis suggests that some parents do misjudge the abilities of their deaf child at the start of high school. If better educated parents underestimate their child's capacities, it may be a result of their developing understanding that their child may not succeed at their standard of living. Less well educated parents may still be reflecting an optimism based on a lack of understanding of their child's real potential. In other explanations of this kind of a discrepancy between parental traits and parental values, the source has often been attributed to an ignorance of the operation of the school system (Seginer, 1983).

PREVIOUS EDUCATIONAL EXPERIENCE

Preschool Experience

For 28% of the subjects, the school programs were unable to provide us with any information on the child's pre-school experiences. The next largest category of subjects were those who had both an oral preschool and an oral kindergarten experience (19.7%). The third largest category were those who had both a total communication preschool and total communication kindergarten experience (16.4%). More students attended preschool than did not attend some kind of preschool program on the basis of the information that was available. Of those individuals who did not attend preschool, 51% attended an oral kindergarten and 34% attended a total communication kindergarten program.

Among the children who had oral educations in both preschool and kindergarten, 71% were in self-contained or special classes for the deaf. Among the children who had total communication experiences in both pre-school and kindergarten, 57% were in self-contained classes. 18% of the orally educated children were mainstreamed without any support services while none of the children with two years of total communication experience were. On the other hand, 38.3% of the total communication children were mainstreamed in some fashion but were mainstreamed with support personnel of some kind. Most of the children who moved from an oral preschool to a total communication kindergarten were in self-contained pre-school classes.

Communication Practices in Elementary School

There were four general types of communication mode histories within the sample. 19.4% of the entire sample had an oral education up through Grade 8. 17.5% of the sample changed from an oral to a total communication program at some time during elementary school. 29.8% of the sample used total communication throughout their entire educational experience. 28.7% had either mixed or incompletely reported communication histories.

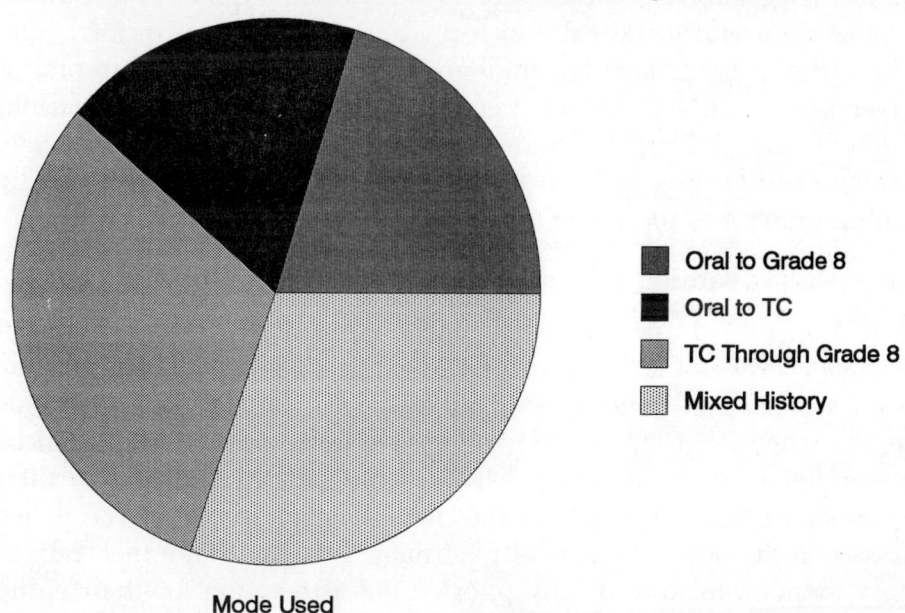

Figure 3.4
Communication Practices in Elementary School

- Oral to Grade 8
- Oral to TC
- TC Through Grade 8
- Mixed History

Mode Used

A multiple regression analysis was computed to predict communication mode use during elementary school based on the set of historically prior variables presented in Chapter 2. Communication mode use in a school program was similar to home communication mode use in that it was predicted by the degree of the child's hearing loss (beta = .185, p < .001); however, it differed in that two other variables, ethnicity (beta = .255, p < .001) and family resources (beta = .140, p < .02) were introduced as predictors. This combination of variables accounted for 12% of the variance. It should be mentioned that family resources includes a component of maternal education, a factor that was earlier found to predict mode use in the home. Degree of hearing loss was directly related to the child's communication mode in elementary school. Orally trained students had an average hearing loss of 77.6 dB (s.d. = 23.1) while students from total communication programs had an average hearing loss of 92.4 (s.d. = 18.5). Students who moved among oral and total communication programs had an average hearing loss of 86.4 dB (s.d. = 21) as measured by better ear average. The relationship between family resources and communication mode use in elementary school was not linear. Students in oral programs and students who moved among oral and total communication programs had slightly below average family resource scores, the students from total communication programs had substantially higher than average family resource scores. White students were more likely to have been orally trained and less likely to have been in total communication programs. Asian students were more likely to be in oral or mixed settings. Black students were most likely to have been in various different settings. Hispanic students virtually always were placed in total communication programs. In fact, the number of hispanic students in oral programs was about one-third of what would be expected.

Early Mainstreaming Experiences

16.7% of the sample spent their entire elementary education in self-contained classes for the deaf. If you add to this the 6.6% of the sample who were in residential schools until junior high, the 2.2% of the sample who returned to special classes, and the students who only experienced non-academic mainstreaming, 44.6% of the sample spent all of their elementary education without exposure to hearing students in academic classes. At the other extreme of placement experience are the 12.3% of the students who were in unsupported mainstreaming for their entire elementary school experience.

To predict elementary school placement, a regression analysis was computed using the same model as that used for predicting communication mode use in school. Elementary school educational placement was predicted by family resources (beta = .211; p. < .001), degree of hearing loss (beta = −.147; p < .001), and ethnicity (beta = −.183; p. < .002). The combination of variables accounts for 12% of the variance. The relationship between degree of mainstream placement in elementary school and family resources is linear with the exception of students who were in supported mainstream placements. The less restrictive an environment the child experienced increases in proportion to the amount of family resources, both income and parental education. For example, twice as many white students were in multiply mainstreamed or unsupported mainstream settings than would be expected.

Summary

Ethnicity, which influences the educational opportunities of deaf children, is reciprocal with family resources. These results suggest that ethnicity as an expression of family resources results in differences in educational placements; however, ethnicity as a social or linguistic phenomenon is probably responsible for the type of communication mode the child experiences.

In other words the family's ability to provide more educational opportunities for the child results in the child having more experience in mainstream classes. White students are more likely to have an oral education and less likely to be in a total communication program. Hispanic students are less likely to have an oral education and much more likely to be in a total communication program. Black students and asian students appear in various communication mode situations about as often as would be expected given their numbers. White students are less likely to be found in special classes and more likely to be mainstreamed. Black and hispanic students are more likely to be in special classes and less likely to be mainstreamed. What this suggests is that school personnel are giving more opportunities for more challenging situations to the children of parents whom they perceive as more "supportive." Over the course of the study, several school administrators made the point that parent involvement or support was a factor in decisions to mainstream children. These results support those anecdotes.

Gender appears to be unrelated to any of the other variables considered so far.

Hearing loss predicts placement history and communication mode use. Less severely impaired students are more likely to receive an oral education. Kluwin and Moores (1985) and others have considered the characteristics of students who are mainstreamed and found that degree of hearing loss which is also related in these studies to other measures of communication ease with hearing people is a predictor of increased mainstreaming.

Placement history is reciprocal with communication mode use. Students who are orally educated are generally encouraged to take more mainstream classes.

Ninth Grade Traits

The primary tool we will use in this section of this chapter is path analysis. Path analysis which is a special version of multiple linear regression often provides illuminating pictures of relationships within a complex data set. However, for the reader who may not be a skilled statistician, let us point out that path analysis is a descriptive statistic. It is a more elegant representation of a complex data set than a collection of correlation coefficients. As a descriptive statistic it is informative but not conclusive. The appearance of a variable does not "prove" a point and must be interpreted with care. The great advantage of this type of analysis is that it does show complicated relationships; however, alternate explanations for phenomenon must be respected.

Figure 3.5
Inter-relationship of Ninth Grade Traits

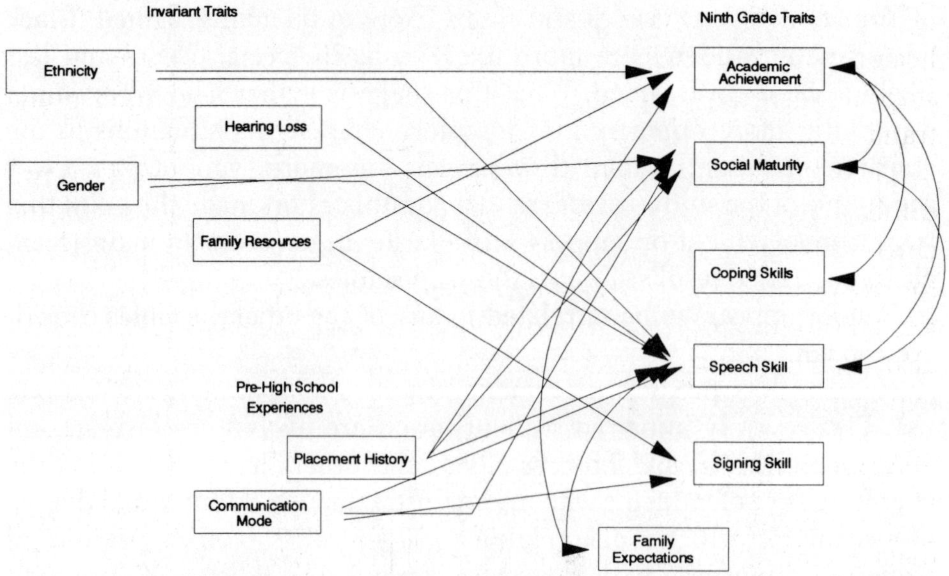

Ninth grade academic achievement correlates with social maturity ($r = .354$; $p < .001$), coping skills ($r = -.170$; $p < .001$), speech skills ($r = .418$; $p < .001$), and family expectations ($r = .293$; $p < .001$). In addition social maturity correlates with speech skills ($r = .215$; $p < .001$) and family expectations ($r = .200$; $p < .004$). Finally, speech skill correlates with family expectations ($r = .176$; $p < .009$).

Reciprocal relationships between the measure of social maturity and other measures must be considered in the context of the source of the data for the social maturity measures. The social maturity measures come primarily from the Meadow-Kendall Social Emotional Assessment Inventory which is based on a school staff member's rating of the student. It is possible that traits valued by school personnel may be influencing the scores and producing some of the strength of the relationship. Consequently, the relationships between social maturity and school achievement and speech skill must be tempered by this influence. At the same time there is a certain logic in that higher achieving students will be more mature and have families with higher expectations for them. Kluwin and Gaustad (1991) make this point about the reciprocal nature of school achievement and parental expectations, particularly during the early elementary years. The reciprocity of higher family expectations and greater social maturity also has an obvious logic.

The reciprocity of speech skills and achievement is probably the result of the cumulative effects of more mainstream education and a lower hearing loss. More will be said of this below when we discuss the relationship between the pre-high school characteristics and the ninth grade traits.

The reciprocity between speech skill and family expectations has two dimensions. First, there are the aspirations of the hearing parents for the child who has more "normal" speech. Second, as will be seen later in the discussion of the relationship between the pre-high school characteristics and the ninth grade traits, factors which contribute to speech skill also contribute to achievement and form a feedback loop to parental expectations.

Academic Achievement.

Ninth grade academic achievement is predicted by family resources (beta = .182; $p < .002$); elementary school class placement (beta = .246; $p < .001$); and ethnicity (beta = $-.165$; $p < .04$). For the purposes of this study, ninth grade achievement is actually a starting point. While it would be interesting and appropriate to know how such factors as performance IQ contribute to ninth grade achievement, we are only interested in ninth grade achievement from the perspective of knowing what factors are already interacting with achievement at the start of high school. No doubt, some measure of general intelligence would be a major predictor of this variable; however, our purpose is to use ninth grade achievement as a control for twelfth grade achievement later in the analysis.

The impact of family resources and ethnicity on achievement are not surprising since it was already noted that family resources and ethnicity are reciprocal relationships. Kluwin and Moores (1989), and more specifically Kluwin (1992b) make the point that such factors as exposure to content and expectations for achievement are different among different types of educational placements for deaf students. The loading of elementary school class placement on ninth grade achievement only reinforces the observation that the more accelerated pace of mainstream classes does contribute to higher achievement. At the same time, serious caution should be taken in not over-interpreting this result since the same literature just cited also argues along with others (Allen & Osborn, 1984) that there are significant demographic differences among class placements including ability differences. The degree to which elementary school class placement in this equation represents student ability or instructional quality is debatable.

In regard to family resources, more affluent and better educated parents have children who have higher ninth grade achievement. In respect to ethnicity, white and asian students are achieving equally but above hispanic students who are achieving above black students in the ninth grade.

Elementary school class placement shows a distinct set of experiences ordered from lowest achieving in ninth grade to highest: special classes only, variable placements, regularly mainstreamed for one academic class, mainstreamed for two or more academic classes, and unsupported mainstreaming. A profile of the modal higher achieving student in the ninth grade would be the affluent white student who has been mainstreamed. The modal lower achieving ninth grade student is the less affluent black student who has been in special classes. A caution here is to note that modal means most frequent and ignores the Asian students of varying economic backgrounds who have generally higher achievement levels; however, even this small group seems to divide into higher and lower achieving students with distinct differences between them.

Social Maturity.

Ninth grade social maturity is predicted by elementary school communication mode use (beta = $-.146$; $p < .008$), gender (beta = $.149$; $p < .001$), and previous class placement (beta = $.214$; $p < .001$). It needs to be noted that it is also reciprocal with academic achievement and speech skill in the ninth grade. Since the social maturity rating system involves, for the most part, adult hearing persons' assessments of deaf adolescents, factors which would appeal to these individuals such as school achievement and ease of communication must temper any interpretation of the results.

Female students are rated as having higher levels of social maturity. On the basis of previous class placement, there are three groups of students: primarily special class placements, students mainstreamed for one academic class, and students with more mainstream experience. For communication mode use, there are only two groups. Those who have had only oral education backgrounds are rated significantly higher than those who have had mixed backgrounds or total communication backgrounds.

Speech Skill.

Perceived speech skill in ninth grade is predicted by elementary school communication mode use (beta = $-.154$; $p < .001$), gender (beta = $.120$; $p < .01$), degree of hearing loss (beta = $-.419$; $p < .001$), previous class placement (beta = $.118$; $p < .02$) and ethnicity (beta = $-.152$; $p < .002$). It needs to be noted that it is also reciprocal with academic achievement and ninth grade social maturity.

On the basis of communication mode used, the groups ranked themselves from highest to lowest as: orally educated, varied communication modes, and total communication programs. Female students had higher self-evaluations of speaking skills. As a student's hearing loss became more profound, he or she was less likely to evaluate himself or herself as having good speaking skills. Elementary school educational experience divided the students into three groups from lowest to highest ratings of speech skills: special class or variable placements, mainstreamed for a single academic subject, and mainstreamed for several academic subjects or unsupported mainstreaming. White students rated themselves as having better speech skills than all minority group students combined.

The composite individual with good speech would be an orally educated, white female with a less severe hearing loss who had been extensively mainstreamed in elementary school. The prototypical individual with poor speech would be a minority group male with a more severe hearing loss who had been in special classes in elementary school. There is a certain tautology in observing that orally educated children had better self-ratings of speech skill. Further, the relationship between hearing loss and self-rated speech skill is logical if not completely obvious. Frequency of contact between English speakers might account for the advantage enjoyed by those who were more mainstreamed. Ethnicity effects are partially explained by the much lower self-ratings of asian and hispanic students, many of whom come from non-English speaking families. Since English is the first language for most black Americans, the low ratings might be explained to some degree as the result of placement history effects, that is, less exposure to mainstream settings and a greater likelihood of placement in a total communication program. It, unfortunately, may also reflect a lower degree of self-esteem on the part of these students.

Sign Skill.

Signing skill is not reciprocal with any of the other variables and is only predicted by communication mode use (beta = .683; $p < .001$) and family resources (beta = .096; $p < .02$). Previous educational exposure to manual communication would appear to be a good predictor of sign language skill and such is the case in this study. Previous work by Kluwin and Gonter (1991) has suggested that maternal education is a primary determinant in the family's use of manual communication. This may be the component of the family resource variable that accounts for the contribution of family resources to signing skill. Since family resources also predicts elementary school communication mode use, there is a latent effect for family resources as well as through elementary school communication mode use.

CAN WE PROFILE OF THE ENTERING NINTH GRADER?

While it would be desirable to produce a profile or some other summary of the entering ninth graders, this is not as easy as it may seem. At least, five variables would be required: ethnicity or social class, degree of impairment, academic ability, preferred communication mode, and degree of mainstream experience. Even simple categorizations of these variables would produce 120 combinations. Our data set produced 99 of the possible 120 combinations, once again pointing out the uniqueness of each deaf child within a local public school program. The most frequently occurring group (8% of the total) were white students, poor or affluent, who were profoundly deaf, achieving above the average and had been through total communication programs and had experienced some mainstreaming. The second most frequently occurring group (6.2% of the total) were poor and profoundly deaf black students with below average achievement in the ninth grade and a history of total communication programs and special class placements. The next three most frequently occurring types, each representing about 3.5% of the total, were less affluent, orally educated white students who were profoundly deaf achieving above the average and had been in some mainstream classes; less able black deaf students who had been in a variety of communication settings and were achieving below the average; and lower achieving hispanic students who were profoundly deaf, had been through total communication programs and had no mainstream experience.

At the start of ninth grade we had a diverse collection of individuals going into a variety of programs. The only way to reasonably think about them is one at a time. However, to keep from becoming totally lost, the most reasonable way to talk of their experiences is in terms of major influences. Consequently, later chapters will address major influences using the individual student as the unit of analysis.

Chapter 4

COURSELOADS, PROGRAMS, AND TRACKING

The cumulative effects of educational practice tend to be compromises between extremes of experience. Put more concretely, in freshman year, a hypothetical student might have had Ms. Stoneheart for English; sophomore year Mrs. Sweet; junior year, Coach Halefellow; and senior year, Mrs. Nitpicker. While the student's experience was bounded by a mania for grammaticality and an obsession with footnoting term papers, the middle years were awash in off-task but pleasant activities ranging from "shoebox sets" for Shakespeare to making pom poms for homecoming. While deaf students tend to have contact with a smaller number of teachers, their experiences can be just as extreme. Nonetheless, the cumulative effect is often some kind of middle ground of possible experiences.

There are also problems from a research perspective with anything more than globally characterizing long term educational experiences since even in short term studies of the effects of educational interventions precisely typifying what happened can be difficult. For example, in three studies of the short term learning of deaf students in local public schools (Kluwin & Moores, 1985, 1989; Kluwin & Kelly, 1990), two problems of operationally defining constructs came up. The first problem involved typifying course content even in a high consensus field such as mathematics (Kluwin & Moores, 1985; Kluwin & Moores, 1989). The second problem was the movement of students among classes and teachers even over a short period of time (Kluwin & Kelly, 1990).

The two studies by Kluwin and Moores (1985, 1989) illustrated two further problems of typifying school experiences. In the earlier study, mathematics instruction was globally defined as participation in a mathematics class. No distinction was made among different major subject matter divisions within mathematics such as arithmetic, geometry, algebra or business applications. In the latter study, courses were typified on a general basis such as divisions into geometry, algebra, and so on in order to derive measures of the amount of homework required in each class. While the study used "objective criteria" by equating the contents of the textbooks, it was apparent that "Algebra I" in Texas was not the same course as "Algebra I" in Massachusetts. Similarly named courses would vary on the range, depth, and pace of content coverage.

In the study by Kluwin and Kelly (1990) an attempt was made to deliver a two year "educational treatment"; however, the fluidity of school populations produced four separate categories of participants: first year only students, second year only students, students who had the same teacher for two years, and students who changed teachers between years. In addition, Kluwin and Kelly reported possible interactions between the type of experience the student had and student demographic characteristics. These real world obstacles make it extremely difficult to operationally define what the experience was.

More careful description and definition of experiences does not appear to be a workable solution. As definitions become more precise, more apparent variation is seen among the students' experiences. A further difficulty is that as smaller units of description are used, the likelihood of effects "washing out" due to variations in patterns of experiences becomes greater. As we will point out later, a more realistic solution is to apply general terms to patterns of experiences. The resolution to the problem is not to think of educational experiences as tightly defined treatments in the traditions of bio-medical or agricultural research but to regard them as collections of interactive although independent traits.

Consequently, in this chapter we will look at the school experiences of these students from a large scale perspective. The level of discussion in this chapter will be on generalized conditions such as degree of mainstreaming experienced and the overall education plan of the students. We will begin our discussion with a description of the relationships among some educationally significant characteristics of deaf students which will be followed by a discussion of who is mainstreamed and who is not based on these traits. Next, we will talk about programs of studies and how these are a critical factor related to degree of mainstreaming which are often ignored in discussions of educational programming for deaf students. Finally, we will discuss who dropped out of school.

Selectional Criteria for Mainstreaming

The educational experience of an individual deaf child is a construction fabricated out of the responses of local conditions to legal requirements set by a national agenda. The placement of a particular deaf child within an educational setting in a local public school is conditioned by the characteristics of the student, the legal requirements of the system, the available features of the program, and the parameters of the placement process. This is perhaps the coldest and most clinical description. Ultimately, these are individual children, each with names and personalities who face the results of this collective wisdom on their own.

Who Was Mainstreamed in High School?

Various sources will tell us that selection for mainstreaming will be on the basis of the following variables in the order of importance: academic ability, social maturity, communication skill, and parental support. What we have noted in our data set is that these are highly related variables. When one school program says it considers only achievement and another says that it considers achievement and maturity or achievement and communication skills when making a decision to mainstream, they are expressing similar values. As we can see from Chapter 3, ninth grade achievement, social maturity, language skills, and family expectations overlap. Family resources or ethnicity along with degree of hearing loss and gender contribute in much the same way to each of the ninth grade traits. This is not to say that these are identical measures, but rather they share sufficient variance that factors which predict one tend to predict the others.

The net effect is not a simplistic kind of determinism that allows absolute prediction from a single data point; but in reality, the net is a clump and scatter pattern that is the curse of the educational decision maker. What this means is that for about half of the students, there will be a high degree of inter-relationship among traits. In other words, there were affluent, white, mildly impaired, grade level achieving females entering ninth grade along with poor, black or hispanic profoundly deaf males who could not read or write. One type will have been through numerous mainstream classes in suburban schools without an interpreter while the others will have been in self-contained classes using total communication. However, there were also students entering ninth grade who on one or several variables ran against the trends. As in previous discussions, we will need to alternate between discussions of factors and the expression of those factors in modal or typical individuals.

The students who remained in special classes throughout four years of high school were considerably less well prepared, were slightly more likely to be male, and were more likely to be minority students than

Table 4.1
GROUP TRAITS IN NINTH GRADE

Variable	Special Class Only	Some Mainstream Classes	Single Class Only	Varied Mainstream Classes	Regularly Mainstream	Total
N	54	34	97	102	35	322
Ninth Grade Achievement	−0.76 (.867)	−0.17 (.738)	−0.40 (1.00)	0.33 (1.07)	0.74 (.928)	−.0.09 (1.08)
Hearing Loss*	85.24 (20.6)	82.15 (23.7)	85.63 (21.1)	86.49 (23.0)	92.00 (24.5)	86.17 (22.3)
Percent Male	59.3	64.7	39.2	50.0	40.0	48.8
Percent Minority	57.4	64.7	58.2	39.6	14.7	48.3

*Better ear average as measured in decibels

would be expected. The same could be said about those who had one or two experiences with academic mainstreaming. The students who were mainstreamed regularly for a single academic class would be differentiated from the other two groups on the basis of gender. Otherwise they are quite similar to the special class students. Ability and ethnicity differentiate the students who are mainstreamed for more than one class from all of the other students.

Class placement in high school was predicted by ninth grade achievement (beta = .238; $p < .001$), class placement during elementary school (beta = .223; $p < .001$), ninth grade social maturity (beta = .160; $p < .002$), gender (beta = .128; $p < .01$), communication mode use during elementary school (beta = .131; $p < .01$), ethnicity (beta = −.118; $p < .02$), and family expectations (beta = .105; $p < .03$).

Ninth grade achievement divided the sample into four groups: special class placement or single class mainstream placements who achieved below the sample average in ninth grade; students who sometimes were mainstreamed for a single class who achieved at the mean in ninth grade; students who were mainstreamed for at least one or more than one academic class per year during high school whose ninth grade achievement was .3 standard deviations above average; and those students who were regularly mainstreamed for two or more classes in high school whose ninth grade achievement was .7 standard deviations above the average.

Prior educational experience was a less powerful predictor because of a "ceiling effect." In other words, children who were fully mainstreamed in elementary school could not be mainstreamed more in high school.

As noted in Wolk, Karchmer, and Schildroth (1982), there is a tendency to greater mainstreaming with age. This trend was also noted in our data. 75% of the students who were in separate classes in elementary school were placed in some kind of mainstreaming during high school. Across the board there was a tendency for a child to be placed in a less restrictive environment in high school than was experienced in elementary school; however, if a child was extensively mainstreamed in elementary school, there were fewer opportunities for "more mainstreaming" in high school. Consequently, the change in placement into a less restrictive setting between elementary school placement and high school placement declines as the degree of elementary school mainstreaming increases.

The modal special class student was a severely impaired minority group male with a second grade reading level. The modal regularly mainstreamed student was a white female with a profound loss who read at or above grade level. A white female with a less severe hearing loss who was below grade level in reading but at or above grade level in mathematics ability was the modal student who was mainstreamed for a single class.

MAINSTREAMING BY SUBJECT MATTER

Academic Experience

Mainstreaming means more than simply putting deaf children into classes with hearing children. It also involves the creation of an overall pattern of an academic history. Such an academic history is not unique to deaf education since traditionally American public schools either tacitly or implicitly have created "tracks" for their students such as college bound, business, or skilled vocational training (Boyer, 1983; Coleman & Hoffer, 1987). This process of creating an academic history for a particular child is, in and of itself, not a negative notion since it focusses and defines the choices that will be available to the child; however, the consequences can be significant.

There is an interesting contrast between special education and general education in the process by which a curricular history is created for each child. For deaf students in local public schools, the process is fairly tightly regulated by the stipulations of P.L. 94-142 and any appropriate regulations covering specific programming requirements. Hearing students in these same schools face a different situation. "How do students decide what they should and should not take? The answer: they do it casually, with little guidance. Curriculum decisions are shaped most decisively perhaps by the program or "track" in which a student is enrolled" (Boyer, 1983, p. 79.). Either specifically by school practice—tracking—or accidentally through the accumulation of specific courses, students in American public high schools fall into three general categories: vocational, general, and academic (Boyer, 1983; Coleman & Hoffer, 1987).

The typical American high school graduate completes three years to three and a half years of English, two years of social studies, one year of math, one year of science, two years of physical education or health, and a variety of state or locally mandated requirements as well as several "electives," often vocational training courses, drivers education, and so on. The most frequently specifically mandated course is American history with state history, government or some other civics oriented course required. Foreign languages fare badly with only 15% of the students taking them (Boyer, 1983).

The general American high school curriculum consists of two peaks with a wide and expanding trough between them (Boyer, 1983; Coleman & Hoffer, 1987). At one end are a small proportion of the students taking some kind of focussed vocational education program. At the other end, are another small and shrinking group taking a college preparatory program. In between, there is the great mass of "general" programs.

> At comprehensive high schools, the academic program is considered the most rigorous; it contains the greatest number of so-called "solids" and the aim is to prepare students for further education. The general program is more open-ended, with few academic courses and great opportunity for electives. The vocational track is for students who plan to join the work force after graduation. Most vocational students complete a core of academic requirements, but they are also are expected to complete about five or six job-related courses. About 11% of all high school students concentrate—take six or more units—in vocational education. However, as we noted earlier, more than three fourths of all students take at least one vocational course as an elective—typing or introductory shop, perhaps. (Boyer, 1983, p. 79).

Differences between the programs are not only in terms of the kinds of courses taken but the amount of course work taken. Academic students take five semesters of mathematics while vocational students take three; academic students take nearly two years of a foreign language while vocational students take none; academic students will complete two to three years of science while vocational students finish only one (Coleman & Hoffer, 1987).

Allen and his associates (Allen, Rawlings & Schildroth, 1989) in a massive study of school to work transition note a similar pattern for students in both residential schools and local public schools with 19% of the students in primarily vocational tracks and 57% in primarily academic tracks. They note considerable variability on the basis of gender, ethnic background, additional handicapping conditions, and school settings. Unfortunately, their distinctions are quite general and cannot be comfortably matched with the Boyer or the Coleman and Hoffer categories. In addition, they did not consider the predictive capacity of these groupings.

Nonetheless, some of the practical implications of this policy can be seen. King (1992) reported that less able or lower track deaf students had higher levels of career awareness than did more able students. She speculated that less exposure to vocational education on the part of the college track students could produce such a finding since they would be less likely to have any additional outside exposure to vocational experiences.

Each year the schools in our study were asked to provide information on the students' coursework. The requested information included the subjects taken, the type of placement the student was in, any changes that might have occurred in the placement during the year, and the final grade the student received.

Virtually all of the students took four years of English, two years of mathematics, two years of social studies, one year of science, two years of physical education, and some kind of vocational education class. Ninth and tenth grade consisted primarily of classes in English, mathematics, social studies, science, physical education and some vocational education. During eleventh and twelfth grade there was greater divergence in the general pattern as students were sorted out into vocational, general, and college bound tracks. A vocational track meant that students moved into more vocational education, less social studies or science, and mathematics that focussed on remedial math rather than advanced topics. College bound students continued to take more mathematics classes; a tiny number took a foreign language; and they took more science classes. A general track meant that the student was not clearly headed for college and was not already locked into a heavy vocational education program. The difference between these students and the col-

Figure 4.1
Courses Taken During High School

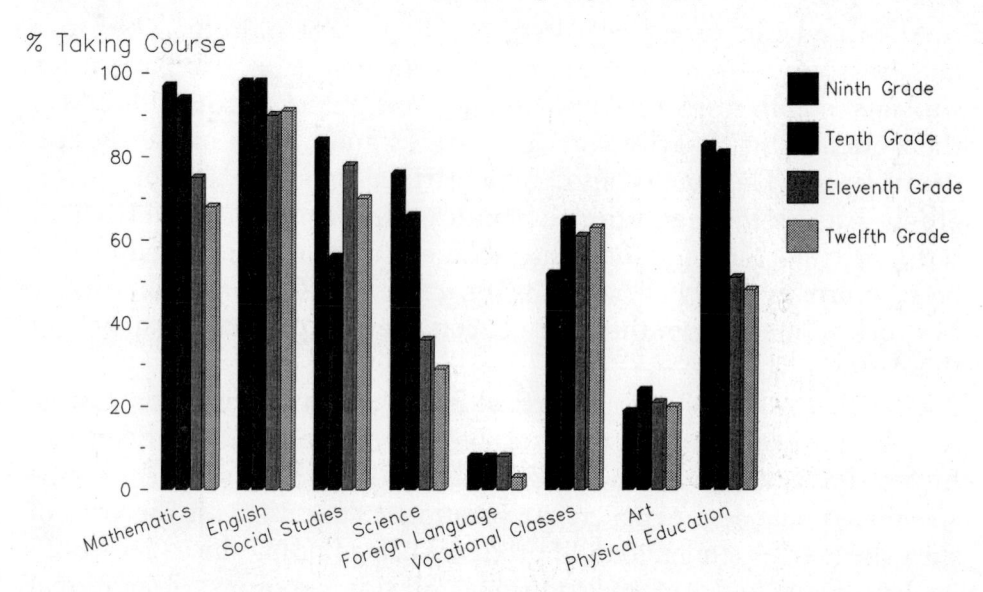

[Bar chart showing % Taking Course for Ninth, Tenth, Eleventh, and Twelfth Grade across the categories: Mathematics, English, Social Studies, Science, Foreign Language, Vocational Classes, Art, Physical Education]

lege bound students was that they got more courses in "career exploration" and some vocational training. The college bound students may have had a woodshop class in ninth grade but did not take any additional vocational training.

Virtually all students took some kind of math class in ninth grade and most took a second class in tenth grade. By eleventh grade, only those students who were regularly mainstreamed or mainstreamed for a specific class, usually mathematics, continued to take math classes at the level they did in ninth and tenth grade. In twelfth grade the only large numbers of students taking math classes were the special class students and the regularly mainstreamed students, but they were taking different courses for different reasons. Special class students spent two years trying to get through ninth grade math. By eleventh and twelfth grade, some were still struggling to get through, but some others had moved onto other kinds of classes. The large number of special class students who took math in the twelfth grade represented two situations. One group of students was still in remedial classes in order to satisfy minimal competency requirements while the remainder for the most part had moved into special topics such as "Business math" or "Consumer math." The regularly mainstreamed students represented the regular progression in

Figure 4.2
Math Classes Taken Over Four Years

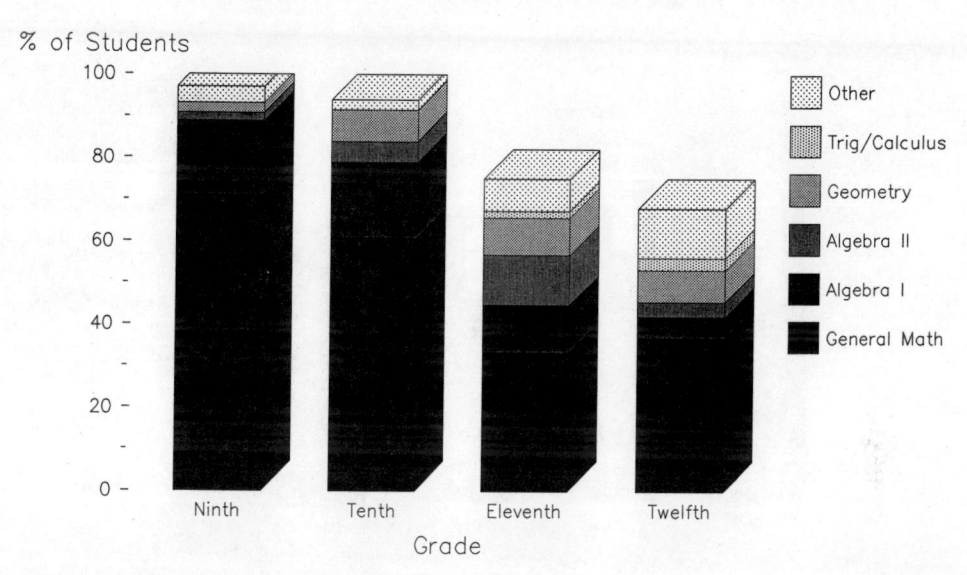

[Bar chart showing % of Students by Grade (Ninth, Tenth, Eleventh, Twelfth) with categories: Other, Trig/Calculus, Geometry, Algebra II, Algebra I, General Math]

high schools from general math to algebra to trigonometry or geometry and eventually to calculus for a minority. The single class mainstreamed students were usually mainstreamed in mathematics. If they did well in a mainstreamed math class one year they were moved to another class the next year. If not they repeated the class, often in a self-contained setting. They would also "top out," that is, run out of math courses suitable to their abilities. This explains why they took fewer math classes but in proportion to the special class students took more algebra to trigonometry level courses and fewer other types of courses. In other words, they had the fundamental math skills, but showed no particular aptitude for more advanced mathematics.

Special class students took more vocational courses in ninth grade than did any other type of students and they continued to taken more vocational education classes throughout high school. The regularly mainstreamed students take very few vocational education classes throughout their four years of high school. The other students fell between these two extremes but increased their percentage of vocational education classes each year.

It was not only the number of vocational education classes that students took but it was the nature of those classes that differentiated among the types of students. In ninth grade, the most frequent type of voca-

Figure 4.3
Vocational Education Classes During High School

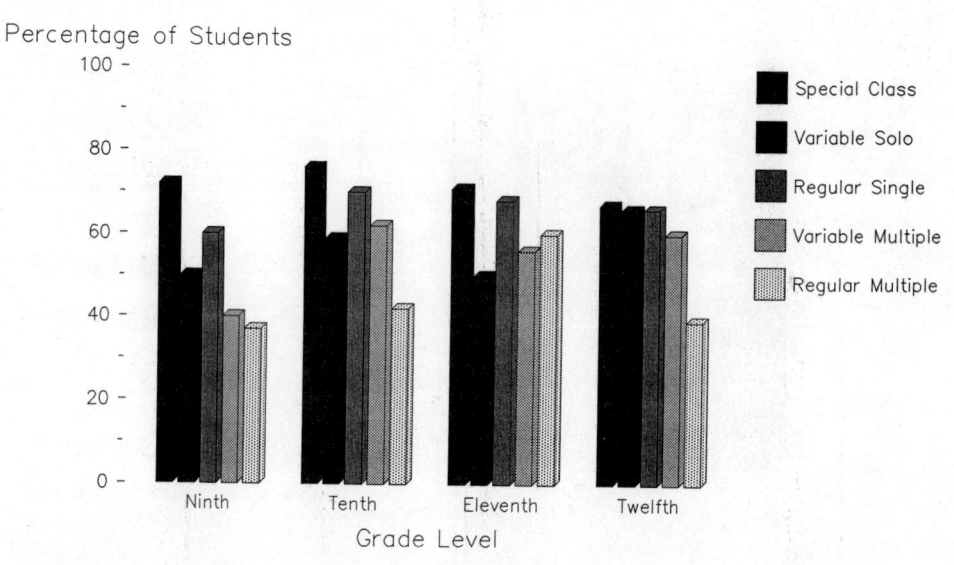

- Special Class
- Variable Solo
- Regular Single
- Variable Multiple
- Regular Multiple

tional education class was some sort of manual arts training such as woodshop or food preparation. After ninth grade, specialization began. For the special class students, vocational training consisted of a large number of manual arts classes, generic "career awareness" or various other specialized classes such as supervised working situations. For the students mainstreamed for a single class, there was still a substantial proportion of effort devoted to manual training classes, but these students also began to get clerical training such as typing or data entry. Very few of the students received any training in service related areas.

Deaf students took very few science classes in local public schools and except for the most frequently mainstreamed who took a very diverse range of classes. The more frequently mainstreamed followed the general school practice of biology in ninth or tenth grade followed by chemistry.

Social Studies courses can be divided into state educational requirements, filler, and college bound classes. State educational requirements tend to be courses in United States history, government, or civics. Filler courses tend to be courses on world history or world cultures where there is a state requirement for a second social studies course in high school. College bound students will also take world or European history courses as well as special courses such as economics in addition to their state

Figure 4.4
Science Classes Over Time By Placement

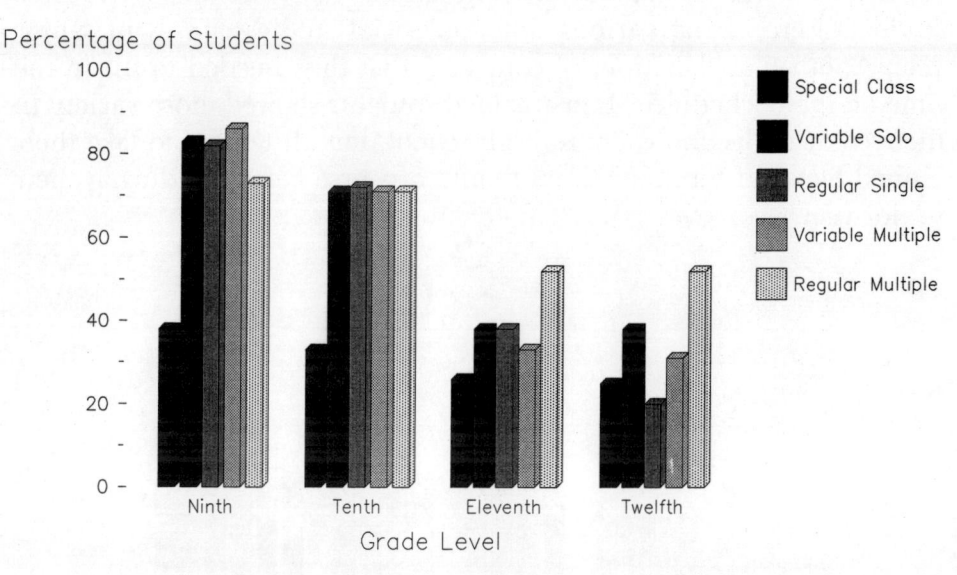

Percentage of Students

Legend:
- Special Class
- Variable Solo
- Regular Single
- Variable Multiple
- Regular Multiple

Grade Level: Ninth, Tenth, Eleventh, Twelfth

Figure 4.5
Social Studies Classes During High School

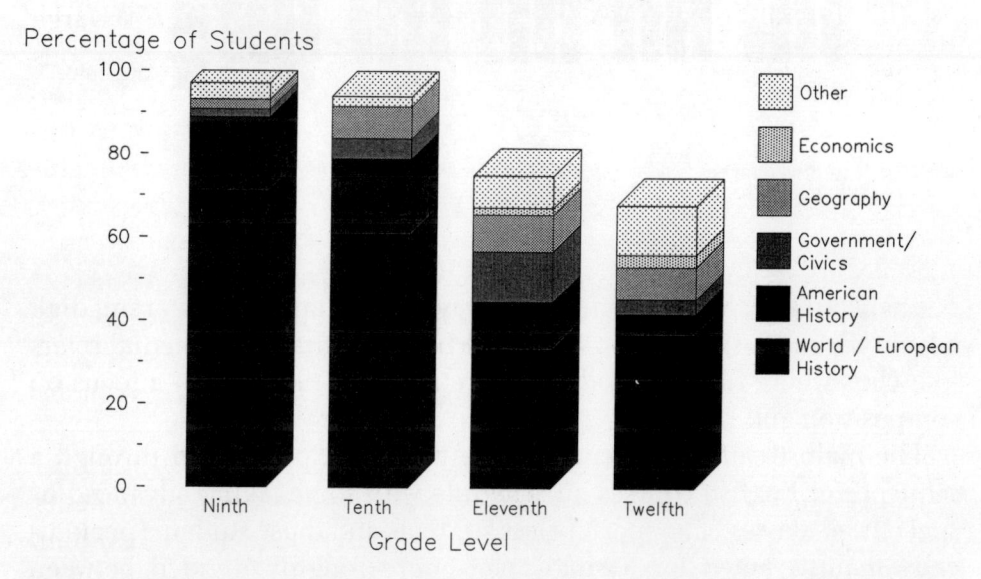

Percentage of Students

Legend:
- Other
- Economics
- Geography
- Government/Civics
- American History
- World / European History

Grade Level: Ninth, Tenth, Eleventh, Twelfth

requirements. While it is not always possible to see specific differences in course content from school records, general patterns are perceptible. The students in the special classes met their minimal state requirements for civics and United States history. In addition, many states required a third social studies course for graduation. This explains why these students were taking various different social studies classes in senior year. Another explanation, of course, is that they needed to fill in the time on their schedule. Mainstreamed students showed more variety in their course selection early in high school, but all tended to take their United States history and civics required course before or during their junior year.

Figure 4.6
English Classes Taken During High School

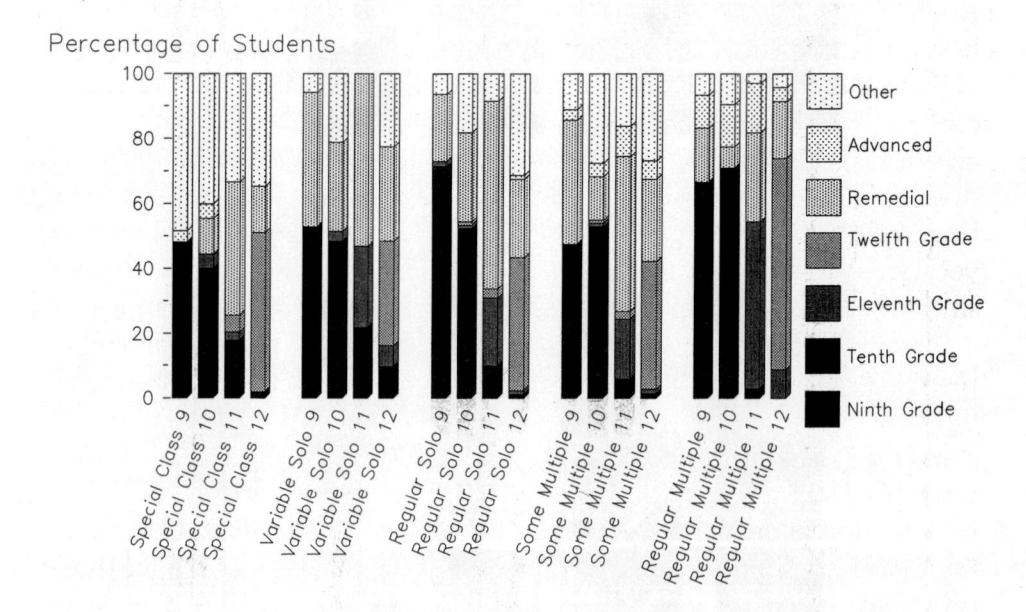

English classes were defined four ways: grade appropriate, remedial, advanced, and insufficiently specific to be categorizable. Remedial refers to a class where fundamental skills are stressed, rather than a focus on composition and literature.

The mainstreamed students for the most part progressed through a sequence of English courses on schedule with some taking advanced or specialized classes. The special class students and those students periodically mainstreamed for a single class were roughly divided between those who took the appropriate course on schedule and those who took a remedial or other kind of English course. One difference between special class students and those who experienced some academic mainstreaming was that with increasing mainstreaming there was less of a tendency to take a remedial class as there was a tendency to repeat a previous year's English class; however, across all groups, except for the regularly mainstreamed students, a minimum of 20% of the students took some kind of remedial English class.

Another way to look at the experiences of deaf students in public school programs is to describe modal course programs. The student who is kept in a special class for his or her entire high school career has a bare bones academic preparation with a heavy emphasis on vocational training in the manual arts. The student who is sometimes mainstreamed for a single class differs from the totally self-contained student in that this student will take some kind of a science and a mathematics course beyond pre-algebra. These students are also likely to receive considerable vocational training with some of the students receiving training in clerical skills. The student who regularly goes into a single mainstream class each year is more likely to take a science and particularly biology in the tenth grade. In addition, this individual's social studies sequence begins to resemble the general education students. Again the amount of vocational training for this type of student is quite high but a further shift toward a larger percentage being trained in service fields appears.

The schedules for the regularly mainstreamed students begin to resemble those of the bulk of the regular school population. The major difference is the continuation of many of these students in special English classes for deaf students. Their schedules are not "college bound," but resemble more those of what used to be termed the "business track," that is, a general educational background with a large dose of clerical training as well as more emphasis on career exploration than the other three previously discussed types. The student who is fully mainstreamed takes a program resembling that of most college bound hearing students. Three to four years of increasingly more difficult mathematics are common. These students tend to be on grade level in English. They take the usual biology and chemistry sequence and often a third science. Their social studies sequence is less important, perhaps because of their greater emphasis on science and mathematics. One large difference between them and other deaf students is that these students take little or no vocational education classes with the exception of typing or computer operations of some kind. They also do not take many courses in career exploration (see King, 1992).

Conclusion

Mainstreaming is not independent of the students' overall educational program. On one level this would be expected because placement decisions are based to a great degree on ability. However, the implications of this process for the discussion of the efficacy of mainstreaming as an educational practice is quite serious. Because an individual deaf student's overall course history is related to the child's degree of integration, it will be extremely difficult if at all possible to disentangle the nature of the contribution of each component.

WHO STAYED AND WHO DROPPED OUT?

Students drop out of school for a variety of reasons including attendance problems in school, lack of interest or boredom, academic problems or poor grades, as well as problems with teachers (Barber and McClellan, 1987; Bond & Beer, 1990; Boyer 1983; Clements, 1990). And sometimes students are simply "lost" from the school record keeping system (Barber & McClellan, 1987; Clements, 1990). Dropouts from general education are marked by low grades, no plans for the future, and a low estimation of their capacity to function in school (Boyer, 1983; Coleman & Hoffer, 1987; Svec, 1986; Finn, 1989). They are less affluent, come from larger families, broken homes, or have more punitive parents who are less well educated (Boyer, 1983; Rumberger, 1987). Additionally, dropouts associate with other dropouts in school (Cairns, Cairns, & Neckerman, 1989). While clearly more minorities drop out (Boyer, 1983; Allen, Rawlings & Schildroth, 1989; Rumberger, 1987), the connection between ethnic status and dropping out may not be as important as the connection between school ability and dropping out (Cairns, Cairns & Neckersmith, 1989; Schulz, Toles, Rice, Brauer & Harvey, 1986).

Deaf school dropouts do not necessarily match national trends as regards some demographic traits. For example, according to Boyer (1983) nearly 28% of starting ninth graders in 1977 did not finish with a diploma in 1981. Coleman and Hoffer (1987) offer a lower estimate of 14.4%. The 14% figure is supported by Cairns (Cairns, Cairns, & Neckerman, 1989). However, Allen and his associates (Allen, Rawlings & Schildroth, 1989) echo Boyer's figure when they estimate that 29% of deaf students who should have exited with a diploma or a certificate dropped out of school. Further, more deaf females and hispanics drop out of school (Allen, Rawlings &

Schildroth, 1989); but based on national figures, more males and minorities in general tend to drop out. Linguistic and racial minorities, males, and the less affluent are more likely to leave public school (Rumberger, 1987).

Who Dropped Out of Our Study

71% of the students who started the study either in ninth or tenth grade in a local public school program had, by the end of the study, either left the program at the same time as those students with whom they started the program or were scheduled to graduate. Another 4.4% had moved on to a similar type of school program and completed that program. 5.1% of the students had transferred to residential schools and had either graduated from those schools or were scheduled to graduate with their peers. There were individual exceptions such as a girl who stayed one year longer to complete extra courses in vocational education, but these situations were counted as completing their high school work. 2% of the students had their placement type reduced, that is, they were transferred from a deaf education program to a sheltered workshop, a program for the emotionally disturbed, or a program for the mentally retarded. 6% of the students were obvious dropouts by the usual definitions. They left school as the result of pregnancy, incarceration, or reached the legal age for leaving school and did not return to finish their diploma program. About 12% of the students simply disappeared from view. Several things happened in these cases. They were reported by their parents as headed for a similar type of program or a residential school but never arrived or the original school or the target school was unable to confirm their arrival. Of these students, it is possible that a considerable number are dropouts, but at the same time, since we cannot confirm their current whereabouts we cannot be more specific about how many are likely to be dropouts.

Why Students Dropped Out

Figure 4.8 presents the reason for leaving the project organized by school program and organized by region. Programs serving only suburban areas as opposed to those serving urban or urban and suburban populations are marked with an asterisk.

The movement of students out of their original programs for whatever reason was primarily a regional phenomenon in that the programs in the Southeast and the Southwest lost more of their original group of stu-

Figure 4.7
Why Students Left the Study

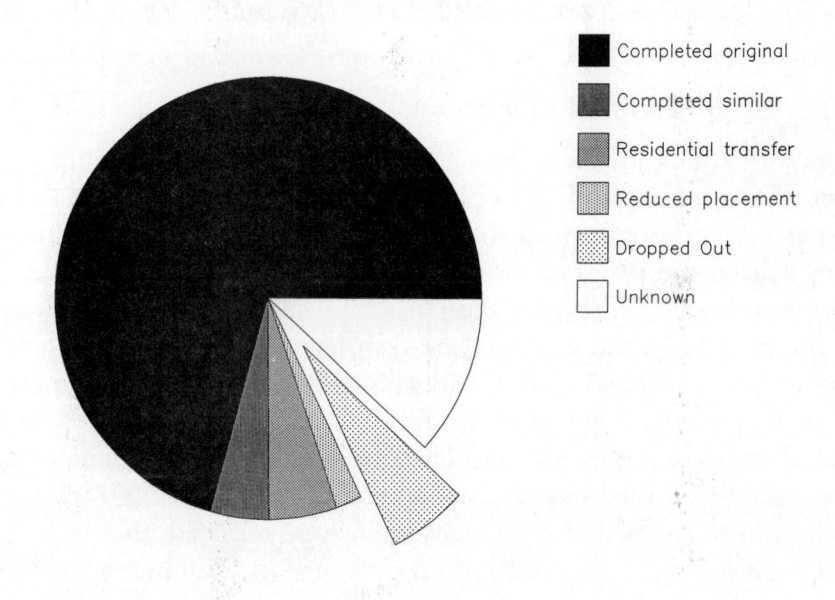

Figure 4.8
Dropping Out By School

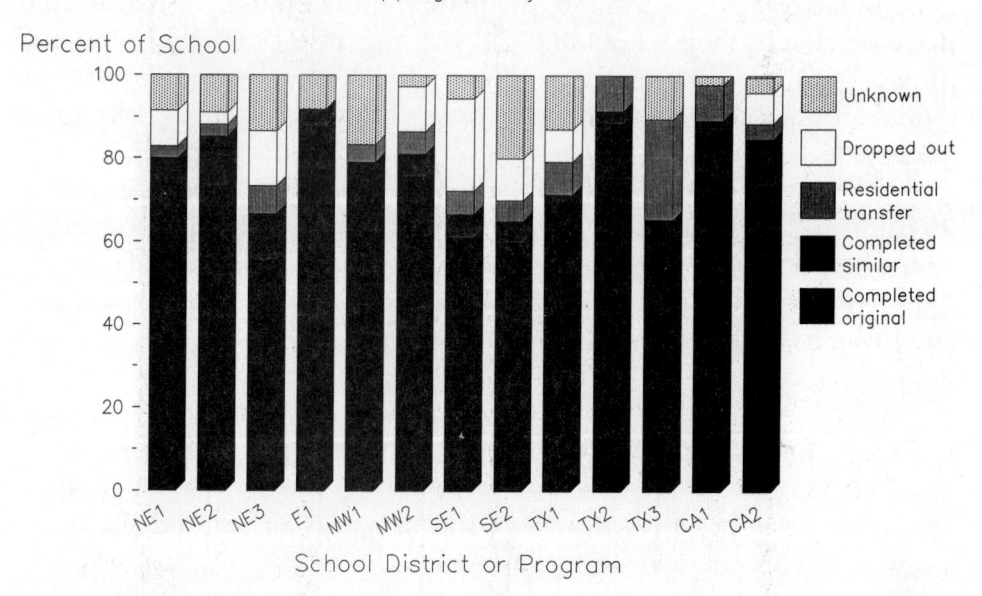

dents than did programs in the Northeast, Midwest or Far West. Leaving a program and completing a similar program was also a regional phenomenon. Programs in the Northeast, Southeast, and Far West were more likely to have students who left their program show up in another similar type of program than in the Midwest or in the Southwest. Transfers to residential school programs were somewhat characteristic of all regions except for the Southwest where it was considerably higher. In fact, one Southwestern program which accounted for only 6.4% of the total sample accounted for 23% of all the residential school transfers. Dropping out was not simply a regional phenomenon but appeared also to be related to urban versus suburban program differences. Unfortunately, detailed analyses of dropout patterns is made difficult by the quantity of unknown situations. Programs that had more unknown situations and drop-outs than the average for the sample were either urban programs or programs in the Southeast or Southwest.

Regional variation is a facet of school attrition nationally. Given the national patterns of attrition plotted against our organization of the sample, the Midwest had the lowest attrition rate followed by the Northeast. In increasing order, the Far West, the Southwest, and the Southeast have attrition rates above the national average.

To consider the impact of individual characteristics on dropping out or transferring to a residential school, a discriminant analysis was computed in which three groups—those who finished in a public school program, those who transferred to a residential program, and those who dropped out—where differentiated on the basis of their ability, degree of hearing loss, race, and gender. Ability was defined as age adjusted ninth grade achievement in mathematics and reading. This was computed using a factor analysis of the students' ninth grade SATHI scores in reading comprehension, mathematics concepts, mathematics computation, and an adjustment for the students' age in ninth grade. Hearing loss was defined by the better ear average. Race was coded as a dummy variable with white students having the lowest value and minorities higher values. Gender was a dummy variable with females coded as the high value.

The analysis produced two canonical discriminant functions. The first function consisted only of the ninth grade achievement measure; the second function consisted of hearing loss, race, and gender. Only the first function was statistically significant with a p value of .03. In this function, achievement accounted for 74% of the variance in group membership. A consideration of the group centroids for both the first and second functions suggested that for those students who remain in a public school program or who move to a similar program—about 75% of this sample—there is no difference between them and the overall sample. This is not a surprising finding given the high percentage of the total sample under consideration. For students who transfer to residential schools, they tend to be the least able students, to be more severely hearing impaired, to be more likely to be male, and more likely to be a member of a minority. Those students who drop out tend to be in the middle of the achievement range, in the middle in the hearing loss range, and less likely to be male or a minority group member than those who transfer to residential schools. Figure 4.9 below presents the three types of student situations broken down by ability quartiles.

Figure 4.9
Program Completion Rate by Ability Group

% Individuals Within the Quartile

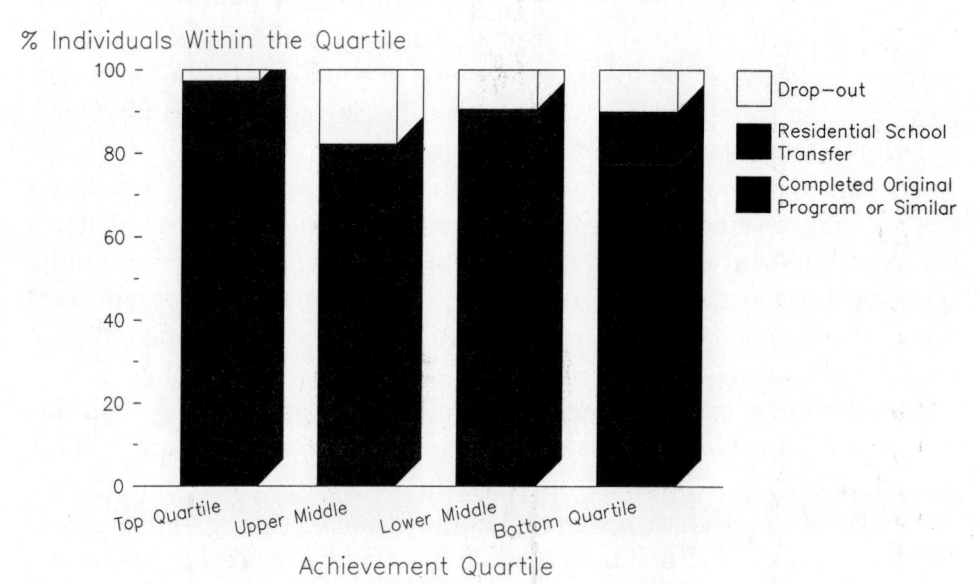

Legend:
- Drop-out
- Residential School Transfer
- Completed Original Program or Similar

Achievement Quartile: Top Quartile, Upper Middle, Lower Middle, Bottom Quartile

Figure 4.9 shows that the bulk of the sample continues on in a program similar to what they started in. It is also apparent from Figure 4.9 that the lowest ability group is the most likely to transfer to a residential school. Dropouts come more or less equally out of all of the ability groupings except for the most able quartile. This observation suggests that a "winnowing" process is occurring during ninth grade where the least able or potential "mainstream failures" are leaving the programs. Several factors could account for this phenomenon including active counseling by the school programs, a rising desire on the part of these students to seek a peer group more attuned to their abilities, or parents' trying to cope with the onslaught of adolescence by seeking more full-time care for the child. Each of these factors can be re-stated as a negative construct, and in the absence of additional information it is not possible to draw conclusions as to the real mechanisms taking place.

Some deaf students in public school programs do drop out; however, the numbers appear to be little different than they are for the general population with many of the same factors at work in the dropout patterns of deaf students in local public school programs including family or community affluence, individual academic ability, and local values toward the importance of schooling.

Chapter 5

INTERACTING WITH PEERS

Adolescents use peer communication in order to try to understand themselves in relation to others through gossip, self-disclosure, problem solving, and an abiding concern with honesty (Gottman and Mettetal, 1986). Honesty among friends, the vulnerability of self-disclosure, the reciprocation of the risk involved in the other's self-exploration, and the ability and willingness to solve personal problems often in terms of the speaker's personality are how the process functions (Gottman and Mettetal, 1986). Adolescents engage in this process of talking about themselves in order to forge an understanding of their own emotions and how these emotions function in relation to other people.

Since peer interaction is an important process in the development of the sense of self, an understanding of the process and occurrence of peer interaction between deaf and hearing peers in local public schools is an essential prerequisite to an understanding of the formation of the personality of deaf students. However, given a repeated picture of minimal to non-existent peer interaction between deaf and hearing adolescents (Antia, 1982; Farrugia & Austin, 1980; Foster, 1988; Libbey & Pronovost, 1980; Raimondo & Maxwell, 1987; Saur *et al.*, 1987), we need to account for the apparent failure of deaf students in public school programs to establish close relationships with their hearing peers (Antia, 1982; Farrugia & Austin, 1980; Foster, 1988; Libbey & Pronovost, 1980; Saur *et al.*, 1987). Two approaches offer some way of accounting for the lack of communication between deaf and hearing peers: adolescent communication research (Gaustad & Kluwin, 1992) and the broader perspective of life history (Foster, 1988).

Gaustad and Kluwin (1992) describe a model of adolescent communication consisting of school activity structure, adolescent trait visibility, and adolescent value systems. Such a model maps well onto our overall analysis plan described in Chapter 1.

School activity structures include all that schools do to create opportunities for peers to interact or the barriers they set up to prevent interaction,

Figure 5.1
*Development of Peer Communication

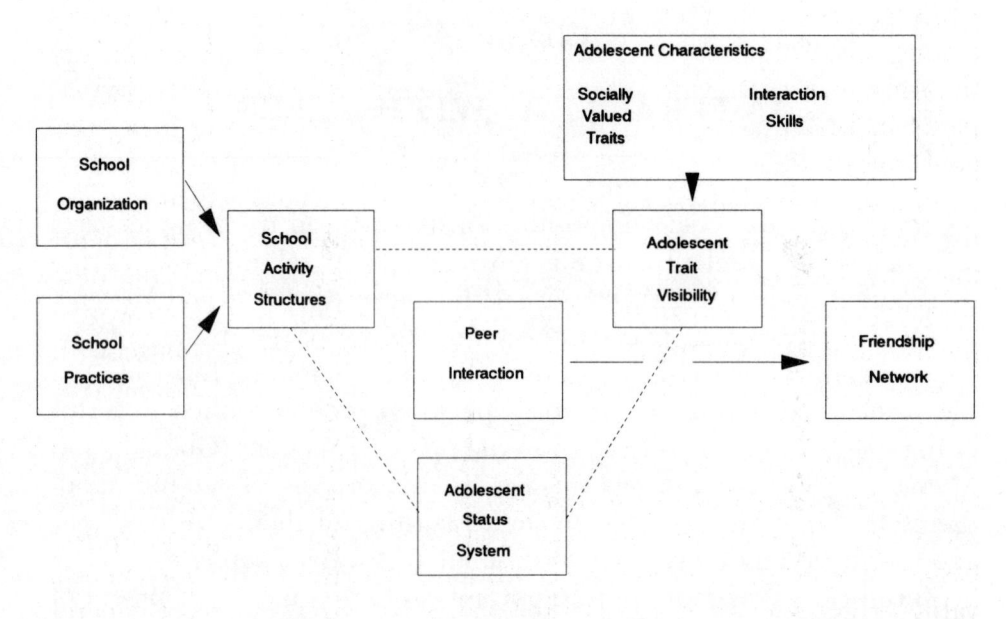

*From Gaustad and Kluwin (1992) p. 111

such as task structures within the classroom (Bossert, 1979) or the use of curricular tracking (Karweit & Hansell, 1983). Adolescent trait visibility arises as an activity draws attention to the characteristics of a student (Karweit & Hansell, 1983). High visibility activities include sports and academic classes while low visibility activities are situations such as the hallways or the lunchroom. The adolescent status system (Hansell & Karweit, 1983; Ingersoll, 1989; Sebald, 1989; Williams, 1975 in Garnica, 1981) means that during interactions, peers set the tone for values concerning clothing, dating, drinking, social events, and club membership (Sebald, 1989). These three elements—activity structures, trait visibility, and status system—define a common ground upon which adolescents can meet. As each adolescent enters this theoretical meeting place, he or she brings with himself or herself specific communication skills.

Ladd, Munson and Miller (1984) in a multi-year study of the social integration of deaf adolescents in high school programs suggest that the prevailing hearing adolescent value systems as well as the perceived affiliation traits of the deaf students are not static. They report that in general the majority of the mainstreamed students experienced greater degrees of social integration and classroom interaction over time. While peer ratings by the hearing students of the deaf students were relatively free of negative factors; they were also broadly distributed which the investigators chose to interpret as a recognition of individual differences among the deaf students by the hearing peers. There were two exceptions to this general pattern. First, deaf students who were early participants in the program were perceived as more considerate than later entering students. Second, later arriving students were evaluated as exhibiting more disruptive behavior. What this suggests is that some of the "novelty" of the deaf students was wearing off. The hearing students may have begun to apply their own peer group criteria to the deaf students rather than regarding them as a unique group. In other words, the deaf students, as time went on began to experience more contact with hearing students and at the same time were beginning to be evaluated as peers.

Affiliation traits or characteristics of the interlocutors which encourage or discourage interaction include gender, common language, and social class. Adolescents, in particular, associate or disassociate on the basis of race, neighborhood, physical appearance, dress, musical preference, value orientation, common social experiences, and degree of general social alienation (Hansell & Karweit, 1983; Ingersoll, 1989; Sebald, 1989; Tedesco & Gaier, 1988; Wilks, 1986). Hagborg (1987) provides a useful insight into desirable affiliation traits within a deaf adolescent social network. Using an extreme groups analysis, he examined the traits of deaf adolescents accepted by their peers versus those rejected by their peers. Deaf adolescents more likely to be accepted by their peers tended to be female, older, more socially mature, and more likely to be recipients of peer messages. He argues that the same sorts of traits observed within populations of hearing adolescents apply to deaf adolescents as well.

Interaction skills involve the adolescent behaving in a way that is consistent with the peer group's frame of reference for that particular activity (Hatch, 1987; Puttalaz & Heflin, 1986). In addition, the adolescent must be able to determine what the group norms are and speak about things that are relevant to those norms (Hatch, 1987; Puttalaz & Heflin, 1986). Affiliation traits and interaction skills are partly inherent in the individual and partly the result of reinforcing experiences. Positive experiences will encourage communication through the reinforcement of certain skills. Unfortunately, while considerable emphasis has been placed on the mode of communication between deaf and hearing peers (Gaustad & Kluwin, 1992; Libbey & Pronovost, 1980; Raimondo & Maxwell, 1984), there have been no reports of the content of deaf adolescents' peer discussions; although Stewart and Stinson (1992) provide some compelling arguments that athletics and extra-curriculars would provide good starting points.

From the perspective of communication research, we are left with a general picture of complexity in the components required to specify the factors that would influence deaf and hearing peer interaction but few studies to draw useful information from in order to fill in the blanks.

Foster (1988), starting from a phenomonological approach, describes a fundamentally similar process. Foster (1988) provides an illuminating range of adolescent and childhood experiences of deaf children in school from the trauma of the young deaf child first being sent off to a residential school without any preparation to the rationalizations of deaf adolescents in mainstream programs over why they cannot become socially integrated. The "problems" of the deaf adolescents in mainstream programs fall into two categories:

1. structural problems, that is, the informant was the only deaf student in the school and was sufficiently different to be noticeable;

2. sublimation or deaf students re-interpret the difficult situation as the result of their own "shyness" or the negative attitudes of hearing peers. While Foster's work provides an illuminating record of reminiscences, it does not give us a sense of the nature of the day-to-day contact of deaf and hearing adolescents or the general background situations that gave rise to the individual experiences. Given the college graduation dates for her subjects, many should fall within the very early years of large scale public school education of deaf students. While this does not mitigate the experiences these individuals had, it does limit the generalizability of the findings in the context of this book.

We can relate Foster's findings (1988) to our overall analysis plan and to the Gaustad and Kluwin (1992) model by saying that she does not provide any specific information about school activity structures, other than residential versus "mainstream" placements; however, she does provide considerable information about the impact of adolescent trait visibility, the adolescent status system, and affiliation traits. In the residential school, the deaf student's trait visibility is a function of non-deafness related attributes; the value system is geared toward adolescent concerns without communication limitations, and affiliations can be based on common interests. In the mainstream program, everything becomes problematic. The most visible trait of the deaf student, from his or her perspective, is his or her deafness. Sometimes, but not always, this seems to be the most visible trait for the hearing students.

What is obvious from Foster's vignettes is that the value systems of the deaf students in the mainstream programs are identical to those of the hearing students as Hagborg (1987) had argued from a quantitative basis: forming friendships, going to parties, shared afterschool activities, and so on. Some of the subjects in Foster's study found this with deaf students away from school while others found it with deaf associates after high school. Very few reported finding it in school with hearing peers. In Foster's analysis, deafness itself becomes an affiliation trait, that is, people associate with each other because they are deaf and deafness is a powerful, bonding force. This is not a new idea since Higgins (1980) and others have documented this phenomenon.

MEASURES OF PEER INTERACTION

Peer interaction can be considered in at least three ways: the mode of communication the student prefers, the preferred interlocutors as measured by the size of the social network or frequency of interaction, and the social focus of peers, that is a preference for friendships inside or outside of school.

We have already mentioned earlier in this book that mode of communication can be speech, sign, some combination of the two, or some other method. Preferred interlocutors can be differentiated on the basis of their hearing and on the basis of the frequency of social contact between peers. In other words, a deaf student can have few friends or many friends and those friends can be deaf, hearing, or both. Consequently, a measure of peer interaction would range from no friends of any kind to many friends, both deaf and hearing with different combinations in between. Social focus refers to the location of peer interaction for the deaf student. Among hearing students, there are those who have friends in school because there are no associates with similar interests in their neighborhood, or there are students who have no friends at school because they are not interested in the school culture and seek companions with similar interests outside of school. There are also students who have separate or overlapping friendship circles in school and in their neighborhood because they are individuals with shared interests in both locations or because a group has moved through elementary school together and has remained in touch in high school. Such is not necessarily the case for deaf students who can be socially isolated at home as well as at school as a result of communication difficulties; however, the patterns are superficially similar: school associates only, neighborhood associates only, associates in both places, and none at all. We will use these three constructs—preferred mode of communication, preferred associate, and social focus—in discussing communication and interaction among peers.

Preferred Mode of Communication

There are two issues involved in discussing a deaf student's use of a particular mode of communication. The first issue is how that student came to acquire a communication mode, and the second issue is why the student uses a particular mode with one peer and not with another. Libbey and Pronovost (1980) in an early study of mainstreamed deaf students, virtually all from oral backgrounds, report a very large percentage of speech use between deaf and hearing peers and unusually large amounts of speech use between deaf peers. Raimondo and Maxwell (1987) reported even larger amounts of speech use among a smaller sample without specification of communication history. Libbey and Pronovost's findings of very extensive speech use, particularly among deaf peers, should be tempered by Woodward and Allen's, later study (1989) where they point out the increasing acceptance and use of manual communication in local public school programs, thus making Libbey and Pronovost's results dated. Raimondo and Maxwell's results appear to be artifactual, that is, they are a product of the use of small programs which tend to have less severely impaired students who would be less likely to sign. Gaustad and Kluwin (1992) point out that program level differences can explain differences in mode use; that is, smaller or more scattered site programs tend to be more English oriented whereas larger or centralized programs tend toward a greater use of sign language, a finding also reported by Woodward and Allen (1989). Consequently, we could expect a tendency to speech use with hearing peers although there is some sign use apparent and a tendency to sign use with deaf peers with some speech use as well.

Use of a Mode of Communication with a Particular Interlocutor

The deaf student has two possible peer interlocutors: deaf or hearing. The deaf student can sign to both types, can switch modes by signing to deaf peers and speaking to hearing peers, can use speech with both deaf and hearing peers, can use sign and associate only with deaf peers, or might employ other means of communication. The deaf student's selection of a particular mode of communication with a peer results from three general factors: the deaf student's sign language use, mainstream experience, and access to school activities (Gaustad & Kluwin, 1992). As we said in Chapter 4, sign language use is predicted by the student's elementary school mode of communication, signing skill, race, social maturity and gender. The mainstream experience variables would include the student's hearing loss, speech skill, current and past mainstream placements, and the school program's commitment to mainstreaming as measured by the percentage of students mainstreamed and the percentage of students in extra-curriculars. School access includes the individual student's extracurricular participation, the distance the student has to travel to school, and the student's after school transportation options.

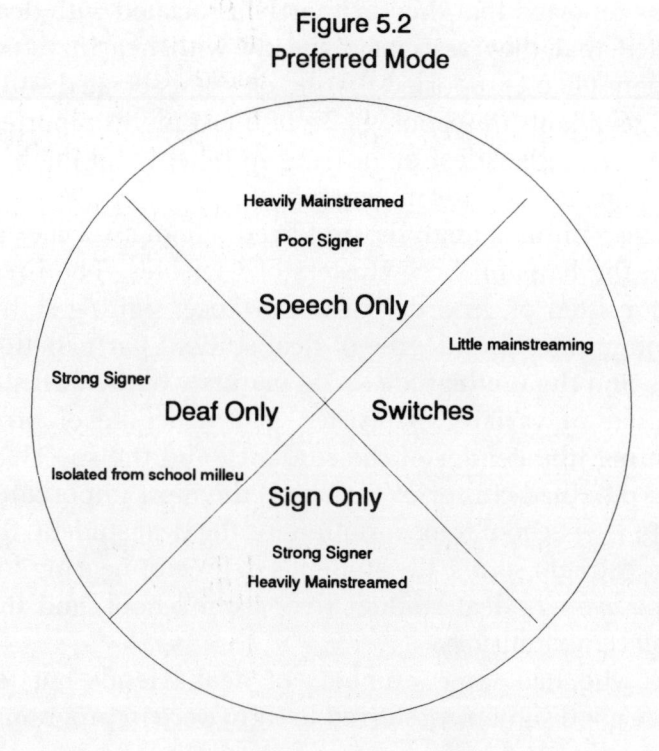

Figure 5.2
Preferred Mode

A discriminant analysis was computed to differentiate among the four types of mode with interlocutor combinations (see Figure 5.2). Students who speak to both deaf and hearing peers have very poor signing skills and extensive mainstreaming experience while access to the school program is not an issue for them. Students who switch from one mode to another depending on their audience have little mainstreaming experience and are undistinguishable on the other two functions. Students who sign in both situations have strong signing skills and considerable mainstreaming experience. Finally, students who prefer only contact with other deaf students have strong signing skills and are relatively isolated.

These findings are similar to Gaustad and Kluwin's (1992) except for the information about the importance of program factors. Gaustad and Kluwin used individual characteristics only in their analysis.

Preferred Associates

A deaf student in a local public school can choose to associate primarily with other deaf students, primarily with hearing students, with both deaf and hearing students, or with neither group. In our study, 29.2% of the students reported that they primarily associated with deaf students. 16% reported that they associated mostly with hearing students. The modal student (40.6%) reported that he or she associated with both deaf and hearing students in school. 14.2% of the students reported that they had few friends, either deaf or hearing in school and the bulk of these reported having few friends in general.

Using a discriminant analysis, preferred school associates were differentiated on the basis of three clusters of variables. The first cluster of variables consisted of, in order of importance, signing skill, preferred mode of communication, degree of deaf student participation in extracurriculars, and the ninth grade social maturity of the deaf student. The second cluster of variables consisted of the degree of program-wide mainstreaming, the gender of the students, and the speech skill of the student. In the third cluster of variables, the most important factors are the access to after-school transportation for the deaf student, the student's current mainstream status, the student's degree of hearing loss, and the distance the average deaf student lives from school, and the student's previous placement history.

Students who had large numbers of deaf friends but few hearing friends were good signers, preferred to sign, were in programs with good

Figure 5.3
Patterns of Preferred Associates

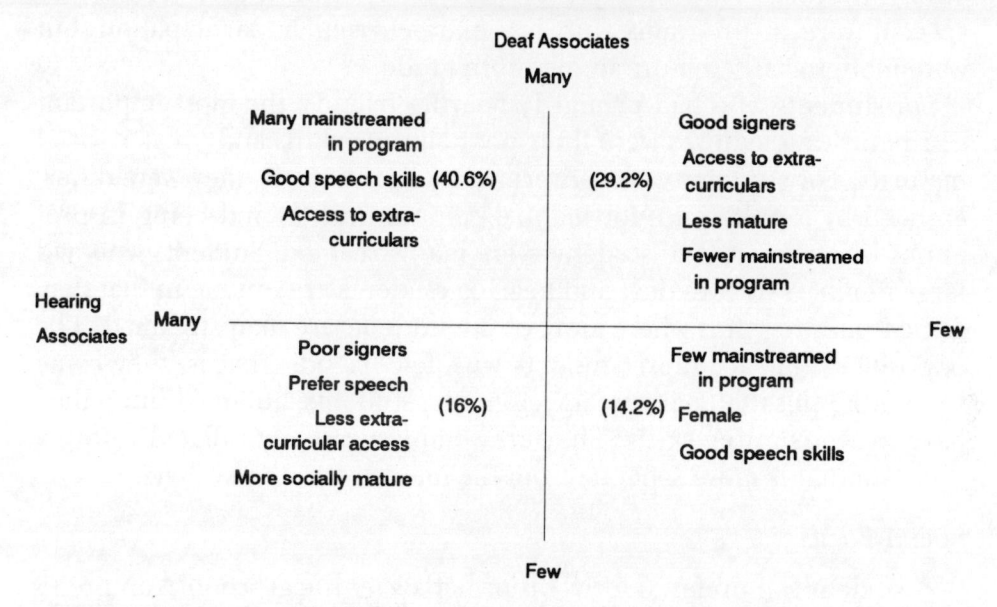

```
                          Deaf Associates
                              Many

         Many mainstreamed              Good signers
             in program                 Access to extra-
         Good speech skills (40.6%)     curriculars
                                (29.2%)
         Access to extra-               Less mature
             curriculars
                                        Fewer mainstreamed
                                            in program
Hearing
Associates  Many ─────────────────┼───────────────────── Few

         Poor signers                   Few mainstreamed
         Prefer speech                      in program
         Less extra-      (16%)   (14.2%) Female
         curricular access
                                        Good speech skills
         More socially mature

                              Few
```

access to extra-curriculars, but were less socially mature in the ninth grade. Further, these students were in programs with fewer mainstreamed deaf students, were more likely to be female, and had poor speech skills.

Students who had large numbers of hearing friends but few deaf friends were poor signers, preferred to use speech, were in programs with less extra-curricular participation, but were more socially mature in the ninth grade. Also they were in programs with a larger percentage of the deaf students in mainstream classes, were more likely to be male, and had good speech skills.

Students who had both deaf and hearing friends were distinguished from other students primarily because they were in programs with a larger percentage of the deaf students in mainstream classes, were more likely to be male, and had good speech skills. Less importantly, they were good signers, preferred to sign, were in programs with good access to extra-curriculars, but were less socially mature in the ninth grade. Other factors do not significantly contribute to differentiating them from other students.

Students with few friends were in programs with fewer mainstreamed deaf students, were more likely to be female, and had good speech skills. Less importantly, they did not have good access to after-school transportation, were less likely to be currently mainstreamed, had a less severe hearing loss, but lived closer to their schools than deaf students in other programs. And finally they were poor signers, preferred to use speech, were in programs with less extra-curricular participation, but were more socially mature in the ninth grade.

For students who had primarily hearing friends, the most important distinguishing features were their poor signing skills and greater social maturity. For students who had primarily deaf friends, they were differentiated by a preference for manual communication and being in programs where fewer deaf students were mainstreamed. Students who had large numbers of both deaf and hearing students are unique in that they come from programs where more of the students are mainstreamed. The opposite of this are those students with few friends, that is, they come from programs that mainstream fewer deaf students, but in addition they have weaker signing skills. They are communicatively isolated within a program that is more separate from the mainstream than others.

Social Focus

A student can prefer to focus his or her social life at school, can prefer to focus his or her social life at home in his or her neighborhood, can have social lives in both places either separately or shared, or may have no particular social focus because he or she has few or no friends.

A discriminant analysis was computed to differentiate among the students on the basis of their social focus: none, school, or both neighborhood and school. We found too few deaf students with a focus primarily in their neighborhood to use in the analysis.

Two functions discriminated among the three groups of deaf students. The first function consisted of, in the order of importance, the percentage of students within the program who were mainstreamed, the elementary school mode of communication of the students, the students' elementary school placement history, ninth grade social maturity, and current mainstreaming status. The second function consisted of the student's access to after school transportation, the distance the student lived from school, the race of the student, and the student's individual participation in extra-curriculars.

The most extreme of the three groups were those who had no particular social focus, that is, they had few friends at home or at school. Students who had neither a school based social focus nor a neighborhood based social focus were characterized by being in programs where

Figure 5.4
Social Focus

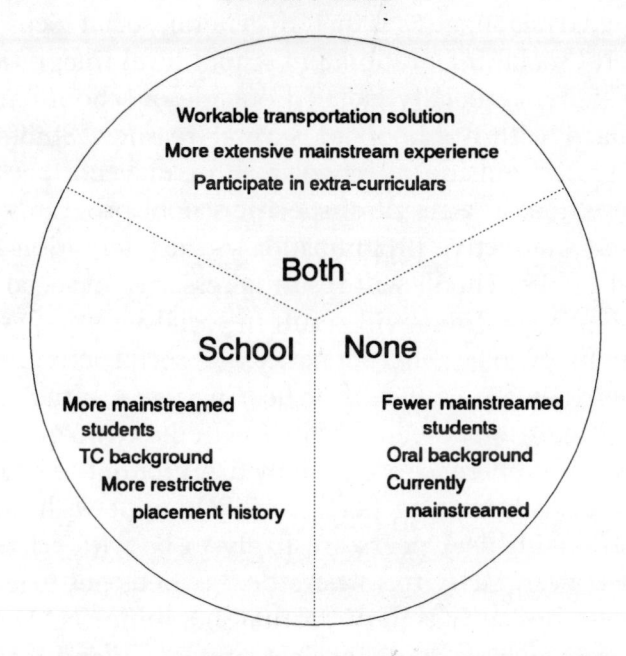

Both
Workable transportation solution
More extensive mainstream experience
Participate in extra-curriculars

School
More mainstreamed students
TC background
More restrictive placement history

None
Fewer mainstreamed students
Oral background
Currently mainstreamed

there was less mainstreaming, they tended to have had oral educations in elementary school, they were in less restrictive environments in elementary school, were more socially mature in ninth grade, and were currently mainstreamed. These students had considerably less flexibility in their after school transportation solutions, lived closer to school, were more likely to be white, and less likely to have participated in extra-curriculars.

Students who only had friends in school were from programs with a greater emphasis on mainstreaming, tended to have total communication backgrounds in elementary school, were in more restrictive placements in elementary school, were less socially mature in the ninth grade, and were less likely to be mainstreamed in high school. The second function did little to differentiate these students from the group averages.

Students who had friends in both school and outside of school exhibited about equal degrees of the two functions. These students were characterized by being in programs where there was less mainstreaming, they tended to have had oral educations in elementary school, they were in less restrictive environments in elementary school, were more socially mature in ninth grade, and were currently mainstreamed. These students had a workable after school transportation solution, lived further from school than the average, were more likely to be a minority group member, and more likely to participate in an extra-curricular activity.

What this analysis suggests is that, in general, social focus is a function of both general social integration and school level integration. In other words, deaf students socially isolated outside of school tend to remain socially isolated within school for several reasons. Students who are socially integrated outside of school may or may not become socially integrated at school as a result of specific school programs. Our results do not suggest that active programs for social integration of deaf children in local public schools will result necessarily in social integration, but failure to provide them will result in social isolation. We recognize that there are likely to be different patterns of social activities depending upon whether they are with deaf or hearing peers, although it was not possible to distinguish between activities with these two given the present methodology. This difference is especially likely for out-of-school activities. While activities with hearing peers are likely to be with neighborhood children, those with deaf peers are likely to be with friends who live some distance away. Activities where deaf friends get together may be structured activities such as participation in a junior NAD club, or may be unstructured, such as apart for deaf students attending various possible school programs scattered through the area, or may be simply having a friend over for a visit, even if that friend lives some distance away.

Summary

The largest single group of students are those who sign to both deaf and hearing peers, have a school focus to their friendship network, and have many friends both deaf and hearing. Another way of thinking about this type of student is someone who has a strong signing background, both in terms of signing experience as a youngster and has strong signing skills. In addition, this individual is probably in a program that mainstreams many of its deaf students, but at the same time has limited after school transportation access. We have not included any measure of sociability in this analysis, but one suspects that these are sociable individuals as well. They have a clear marker of deaf affinity in their strong signing skills but at the same time have access to hearing students through a program level investment in mainstreaming and an access to extra-curriculars.

The second largest group of students are those who change modes as is appropriate to deaf and hearing peers, have a school focus to their friendship network, and have many friends both deaf and hearing. Many of these students got off to a rough start in school in the sense that they are more likely to have moved from an oral program to a total communication program; however, at the moment, they are in programs that are largely mainstreamed and have access to both deaf and hearing peers inside the school program. This suggests that they live a distance from school and do not have good transportation alternatives.

The third largest group of students are those who change modes as is appropriate to deaf and hearing peers, have a school focus to their friendship network, and have mostly deaf friends. A combination of earlier negative experiences with schooling and fewer institutionalized contacts with hearing peers characterizes this group. In a sense, they have been "burned" once and now in a school setting which does not offer large numbers of opportunities for contact with hearing peers, they have focussed their relationships on deaf peers. Beyond these three groupings, numerous individual combinations can be found.

CONCLUSION

There are two ways to think about the formation of peer communication networks for deaf students in local public schools. The first is to think of forces, factors, or variables that create or influence these networks. The second is to think of typical or modal types of individuals who represent groups of similar individuals. As we conclude this chapter we will do both.

All of the invariant traits—ethnicity, hearing loss, and gender—as well as pre-high school experiences that shape communication modes and provide experience with hearing peers influence to some extent the formation of adolescent communication networks. Program level variables sometimes influence social networks but some of these traits may be mitigated by other factors such as transportation alternatives. In general, access to a peer increases the likelihood of forming an association with a peer. Individual experiences during high school which are influenced by invariant traits, pre-high school experiences, and the characteristics of the program also influence the construction of peer networks. Again, more individual access to peers increases the size of the network while the complexity of the contacts increases the complexity of the network.

Looking at individuals instead of forces, students with large networks have had many opportunities for social contact. Students who have complex social networks have physical access to both school programs and the neighborhood.

In looking at individuals instead of forces, we can see where the responsibility of the school program lies. Access is the fundamental underlying issue. It can be defined as communication mode in that deaf peers will require some form of signed communication and hearing peers will require some form of English. It can be defined as physical and temporal opportunity. While putting deaf and hearing children side by side is not a guarantee of integration, the absence of contact is a guarantee of segregation.

The responsibility of the school program lies in the creation of opportunities for contact. In our study, opportunities took the form of the availability of interpreters for extra-curricular events, signing choirs that make sign language a value for hearing students, and available transportation alternatives for deaf students who wished to participate in extra-curriculars.

The school programs could not require these deaf students to develop large and complex social networks even if such were a universal goal. However, some situations were better for producing large and complex networks than were others.

Chapter 6

PARTICIPATION IN EXTRACURRICULAR ACTIVITIES

Since the late 19th century extracurricular activities have had a significant presence in American schools (Gutowski, 1988; Stewart & Stinson, 1992) because extracurriculars provide experiences for students that are important for enhancing their total development that are not provided in classroom learning. Development into adults who function successfully in society requires more than academic learning, and schools bear a large share of the responsibility for developing their students into young adults who can participate effectively in society. Nonacademic programs provide experiences for acquiring skills such as organizing, planning, time-management; for developing personal characteristics such as self-esteem, self-regulation, and motivation; and for fostering social skills such as interpersonal communication, empathy, and leadership (Holland & Andre, 1987).

While there has been recognition of the importance of extracurricular activities among educators of the general population, there has been little discussion of this area, at least in print, with respect to deaf students attending public schools. As schools have attempted to respond to the guidelines of Public Law 94-142, they have focused primarily on academics; issues such as language development, communication mode, academic achievement, support services, and instructional strategies have been at the forefront of discussion (Stewart & Stinson, 1992). There has been much focus on the appropriate placement of the deaf child in the public school into regular or special classes, but little consideration with what happens to the child in the hallway, lunchroom, or after school. This lack of consideration has occurred in spite of strong statements that public school programs have failed to provide adequate extracurricular activities for their deaf students (e.g. Lane, 1992). Garretson, a deaf writer, in 1977 blasted the quality of experiences of mainstreamed deaf students in extracurricular programs, noting that the deaf participant will generally, "tag along as a wallflower, a silent member of the crowd, present and yet absent, second-class participant with latent leadership abilities underdeveloped and dormant without much of a chance to contribute (Garretson in Jacobs, 1989, p. 69)."

There has been recognition that there needs to be more attention to the development of the whole person that extends beyond the classroom and that this focus includes extracurricular activities (Stewart & Stinson, 1992). The 1988 report of the Commission on Education of the deaf stated:

> A child who is deaf should be placed where his or her needs can be met by meaningful participation in after-school or extracurricular activities. This is typically more significant for older children of secondary age who need to learn mature social relationships and behavior (p. 22).

Thus, it is clearly important that public school programs provide extracurricular activities for their deaf students that facilitate their "all around" development.

This chapter is divided into two parts. In the first part we elaborate on why it is important for educators to devote attention to the participation of deaf students in extracurricular activities at public schools. In addition, this section includes a consideration of some of the special issues that educators must address to ensure that deaf students enjoy a quality experience when participating in extracurriculars. There is also at the beginning a brief description of features of extracurricular activities in the American high school. In the second part of the chapter we discuss what we learned about participation in extracurricular activities among the students in the longitudinal study. We present findings from the study and consider implications regarding the quality of experience students may be having and the factors that determine who is likely to participate and who is not.

IMPORTANCE OF EXTRACURRICULARS

Unique Features of Extracurricular Activities

What are some of the features of extracurricular activities that make them special experiences in school? Like classroom activities and related academic programs, extracurriculars are formally controlled and school sanctioned (Karweit, 1983). In contrast to academics, participation in extracurricular activities is voluntary; participants select the activity because it fits their purposes and interests. Thus, in order to continue to exist, the activity must be able to steadily draw a minimum number of volunteer participants. Because of the voluntary nature of extracurriculars, there is a self-selection of interested students. Whereas, in the classroom, students may or may not be interested in the learning activities, in extracurriculars, all students are interested in a particular activity and share the interest with each other (Karweit, 1983).

Another feature of extracurricular activities in the American high school is that they tend to draw a wider range of students in terms of aptitudes, interests, and skills; furthermore, these activities provide greater opportunity for expression of these diverse skills and interests than is true in the classroom. The high school student of today has a tremendous array of extracurricular activities to choose from, ranging from athletics to music to drama to student government, and the number of choices at a particular high school is often in the hundreds. Thus, the talents and behaviors called for by one extracurricular activity are usually very different from those called for by another activity. This diversity contrasts with the typical classroom where display of particular skills and interest outside those specific to the instructional goals of the teacher can disrupt the teacher's effort to coordinate the attention and activities of a large group of students (Karweit, 1983).

Benefits of Extracurricular Activities

At least six benefits of participation in extracurricular activities have been recognized: Participation is enjoyable in itself; certain social and cognitive skills are enhanced; development of personal character is facilitated; academic achievement may be promoted; sense of participation or belonging is heightened; social recognition increases; and socialization into the Deaf community may be promoted.

Enjoyment.

It has been assumed that one reason extracurriculars are so popular at the high school level is because of their enjoyment and entertainment value (Karweit, 1983), which has been noted specifically for drama (Beales & Zemel, 1990) and for athletics (Kirsh, Ham, & Richards, 1989).

Social and Cognitive Skills.

Cooperation is one social-cognitive skill that has been repeatedly recognized as an outcome of extracurricular activities (Griffen, 1988;

Beales & Zemel, 1989; Holland & Andre, 1987). This development of cooperation extends to positive racial attitudes and relationships (Holland & Andre, 1987). Improvements in students' self-awareness, attitudes towards others, communication skills, and interpersonal behaviors have been related to students participating in drama (Beales & Zemel, 1989). Opportunities for development of leadership have been noted as well.

Personal Character.

In addition, participation in extracurricular activities has been associated with increased self-esteem, higher educational and occupational aspirations, increased ability to distinguish reality from fantasy, increased ability to delay impulsivity, and decreased feelings of high school and societal powerlessness (Andre & Holland, 1987; Beales & Zemel, 1990; Griffen, 1988).

Academic Achievement.

Another beneficial outcome of participation in extracurricular activities is greater educational attainment. There is a stronger relationship between participation in athletics and educational attainment for girls than for boys. There appears to be a strong relationship between participation in extracurriculars and educational attainment in activities other than athletics for both boys and girls. Furthermore, students who participate in extracurriculars show lower rates of delinquency than those who do not. One reason for the greater educational attainment of those who participate in extracurriculars may be that the experience helps establish a positive relationship and a sense of integration with the school and its staff that the student would not otherwise enjoy (Holland & Andre, 1987).

Social Recognition.

For the high school student, whether hearing or deaf, an important way of gaining visibility, recognition and status from one's schoolmates is through participation in extracurricular activities. This recognition is viewed by students as an important means to gaining popularity (Holcomb, 1990; Karweit, 1983). For example, "star" male athletes often enjoy wide popularity among schoolmates. Students do in fact assign higher ratings of status to peers who participate in extracurricular activities than to those who do not (Karweit, 1983); furthermore those who participate in extracurriculars view themselves as having higher status among peers than those who do not participate. In addition, students who participate in many activities during the high school year enjoy greater prestige than those who participate in only one (Holland & Andre, 1987). Popular students tend to be joiners who play an active role in many different school activities (Holcomb, 1990).

Sense of Belonging and Friendship.

Yet another benefit is that students enjoy a greater sense of participation or belonging, along with increased possibilities for friendship. Being a member of a sports team, a drama club, or another school group provides a "sense of belonging" for many students more consistently than does the classroom or informal groups in the school hallways (Griffin, 1988). Since participants in extracurriculars have common interests, skills and personalities, chances of friendships developing or being maintained are increased since these attributes are likely considerations in the selection of friends. The extracurricular setting provides good opportunities for participants to learn about each other and to find characteristics of common appeal that can foster friendship (Karweit, 1983). Participation in sports was a major way that one of us, who is deaf and who was mainstreamed in a public school, developed friendships. There was great involvement in the high school baseball and basketball programs. In these programs, it was possible to handle most of the communication requirements and there was extended contact with teammates who shared the same commitment to the sports. Sports programs were relied on for establishing friendships because they provided a means for overcoming the communication barrier and because they provided a quick way of establishing contact when one is new to the high school, having recently moved from another city.

Results from research conducted in England on deaf students who were mainstreamed in public school programs suggests that they, like hearing students, use extracurricular, or structured, activities as a basis for developing friendships. Deaf and hard of hearing students who were involved in structured, that is formal, officially sanctioned, sponsored activities out-of-school also tended to participate in unstructured activities in-school and out-of-school (Stewart & Stinson, 1992; Stinson & Whitmire, 1990; Stinson & Whitmire, 1991). For example, adolescents who reported being members of community-based drama groups or sport clubs (structured) were also likely to report relatively frequent participation in social activities such as visiting friends at their homes or dating (unstructured). This finding occurred for social activities involving deaf, hard of hearing, and hearing peers. On the other hand, involvement in structured activities in-school was not significantly related to participation in unstructured activities. This lack of relationship is surprising, and may have reflected a low emphasis on extracurricular activities in most secondary schools in England. It appeared that involvement in structured activities out-of-school resulted in positive social experiences. Students with this kind of experience were more likely to be involved in informal social relationships with their peers. Therefore, structured social activities appear to be a means by which deaf or hard of hearing students develop closer relationships (Stewart & Stinson, 1992).

Socialization into the Deaf Community.

A final outcome, one that is unique to the deaf students, is socialization into the Deaf community. The image of a single deaf student going into an extracurricular activity with many hearing school mates and no deaf ones often does not hold. While in their lifetimes deaf and hard of hearing individuals frequently interact with hearing persons, they commonly spend a great deal of time relating to other deaf and hard of hearing individuals. For a substantial portion of deaf adults, most of their social life revolves around activities of a Deaf community. Extracurricular activities that have a number of deaf students or that focus on cultural aspects of deafness can help deaf students incorporate norms and values of the Deaf community and develop an awareness of the social options available in that community (Janesick & Moores, 1992; Stewart, & Stinson, 1992). The socializing role of extracurricular activities specifically for deaf students has long been recognized in America, and since at least the late 1800s, residential schools for the deaf have provided extracurricular activities for their students. With the recent increase in enrollment of deaf students in public school programs, more and more of these students have found their way into the extracurricular activities offered at the local school. An increasing portion of athletes participating in Deaf sports at the national and international levels have backgrounds of competing in public school athletics as opposed to residential schools for deaf students (Gannon, 1981; Stewart & Stinson, 1992).

Extracurricular activities designed with deaf students in mind may explicitly deal with the socialization aspect and focus on Deaf culture,

American Sign Language, Deaf heritage or some activity designed to increase awareness of Deaf culture and one's pride as a deaf person. Other activities, such as a sport team or photography club, can provide opportunities for deaf students to get together without focusing so explicitly on the socialization aspect (Stewart & Stinson, 1992).

Participation in extracurricular activities in which there are deaf peers is an important means by which deaf students have contact with each other. In the study of deaf students in England who were mainstreamed, students reported having many out of the classroom contacts with deaf peers, with many of these contacts being with friends from different schools. Afterschool activities can provide an opportunity for deaf friends to get together from within the school offering the program, and from other schools as well. Such contacts with deaf peers seem to be especially important to students who rely on sign language and who are enrolled in schools with few other deaf or hard of hearing pupils (Stinson & Whitmire, 1991).

For these several reasons, then, it is important that deaf students in public schools be able to participate fully and meaningfully in extracurricular activities. Deaf students should be able to participate at least as frequently as hearing peers and their experiences should be as positive as those of their hearing peers.

CHALLENGES FOR DEAF STUDENTS PARTICIPATING IN EXTRACURRICULAR ACTIVITIES IN PUBLIC SCHOOLS

While it is clearly desirable that deaf students be able to participate in extracurricular activities, and there have been increasing numbers of such students participating in such activities in public schools, they have encountered significant barriers to participation whose consequences have ranged from making participation impossible to permitting participation, but resulting in a less than satisfactory experience. Three major barriers have been (a) transportation home for after-school extracurricular activities, (b) difficulties in communicating with hearing peers, coaches, and sponsors, (c) and attitudes among hearing peers and coaches that are insufficiently supportive to make deaf participants feel welcomed or confident.

As we have shown in earlier chapters, special programs for deaf students tend to draw students from a number of school catchment areas in order to provide a sufficient nucleus for the program and this means that most students need to be bused a considerable distance in order to be enrolled in the program. Thus, if a student wishes to stay after school to participate in an extracurricular activity, special busing arrangements must be made, parents must pick up the child, or the student must have his own transportation, in any case traveling a much longer distance than the hearing student typically does. If no arrangements can be made for transportation, students cannot participate in the extracurricular activity, irrespective of their desires to do so (Moores, 1992; Stewart & Stinson, 1992).

Evidence that it is critical for students to be provided transportation home after school is provided in a study by Holcomb (1990). He interviewed deaf and hearing first-year college students about their experiences in extracurricular activities during high school. All the deaf students had been enrolled in mainstreamed programs. The deaf students stated that they were unable to participate in after-school activities because they did not have a ride home much more often than did the hearing students.

Extent of participation in extracurricular activities also depends on the extent to which effective communication is possible with peers, sponsors, and coaches. If deaf students perceive themselves as not having sufficient oral skills to communicate with hearing participants, if hearing participants do not seem knowledgeable about or appear unwilling to communicate with the deaf participants, or if interpreters are difficult to obtain, deaf student may simply refuse to participate. An indication of how this happens is found in Holcomb's (1990) study in which students cited communication difficulties as a barrier to participation. One student commented:

> "I wish I had participated more in school activities, and they are all hearing people who did not know how to communicate with deaf people well enough.... the one thing is problem in communication (p. 90)."

Another student expressed frustration with not having good enough oral skills to communicate with hearing peers during the activity and having difficulty obtaining an interpreter:

> "I did not feel comfortable a lot of time because I don't have communication skills with the hearing. Plus, I felt that the hassle of getting an interpreter wasn't worth it for participating in high school activities (p. 90)."

A report by Mertens (1989) also underscores the importance of communication access for participation. She found that students who reported negative experiences in hearing schools indicated that difficulties with communication interfered with attempts to participate in extracurricular activities.

The study of mainstreamed secondary students in England provides evidence that the support of an interpreter is important for participation when the activity involves interaction with hearing peers and the deaf student relies on sign language for communication. Deaf students who frequently participated in extracurricular activities at school were more likely to have an interpreter than those who participated infrequently (Stinson & Whitmire, 1990; Stinson & Whitmire, 1991). As would be expected, this dependence on the interpreter to facilitate communication in extracurricular activities occurred only for the students who preferred sign language rather than oral communication. Students who reported using oral communication tended not to use an interpreter in extracurricular activities.

Another factor that can influence the frequency that deaf students participate in extracurriculars is the extent that they perceive hearing peers, coaches, and sponsors as having positive attitudes. Particularly in situations where only one or two deaf students are participating, these students may lack the confidence to become involved unless they perceive clear signs of support and friendliness from the hearing members. In Holcomb's study (1990) deaf students in mainstreamed programs indicated that they did not participate in activities because they did not have confidence in themselves significantly more often than hearing students had confidence in themselves. Not having friends in the activity or not knowing others appeared to hinder participation, as deaf students did not report joining an activity along with friends as frequently as did the hearing students. Quotations from Holcomb's subjects revealed that they sometimes (at least) perceived extracurricular activities as a situation where they did not know anyone and where no one had encouraged them:

"I was feeling lonely because no one seems to ask me to participate (p. 90)."

"I would have participated, but due to lack of encouragement, was unable to participate (p. 90)."

While feelings of confidence may result from the support of hearing peers, the adult sponsor or coach has as great if not a greater impact. A few years ago one of us was involved in a survey of deaf participants from the National Technical Institute for the Deaf (NTID) in varsity sports at the Rochester Institute of Technology, of which NTID is one of its nine colleges (Hopper & Stinson, 1987). While the deaf varsity athletes had many positive things to say about their coaches, they also expressed frustration. Some felt they had not received their fair share of attention from the coach, as the following comment revealed:

> "Yes, I did get along with my coach but he didn't enough teach me a skill. He always work with hearing. I don't like it a little (p. 1)."

Another student commented that the coach did not recognize her talents or give her fair playing time because of lack of comfort with having a deaf member on the team:

> "My first year on the team. The coach didn't really care how good I was, he sort of played his favorite players he trusted. He didn't trust my deafness and abilities. I was underrated (p. 3)."

Too much emphasis can be put on these negatives, and it should be recognized that there have been many examples of successful participation in extracurriculars by deaf students in public schools. Still we are personally aware of many deaf persons who have experienced similar frustrations, including the deaf coauthor of this book, in extracurricular activities, especially athletics.

PARTICIPATION IN EXTRA-CURRICULAR ACTIVITIES

Clearly, participation in extracurricular activities is a popular activity among high school students in America, and there are numerous benefits to be derived from participating. It is also apparent that deaf students in public schools can face significant barriers to participating in a meaningful and enjoyable way. What did we learn about participation in extracurriculars among the students in the longitudinal study? We addressed the following questions: (a) How much did they participate in extracurricular activities? (b) What types of activities did they participate in? (c) What program factors, such as the extent students were mainstreamed, were related to level of participation? (d) What were the differences between students who participated in many activities and those who participated in none or few? (e) Why did some students participate in other kinds of activities (e.g. drama)? In this section of the chapter we present findings pertaining to these questions, make inferences regarding how the students experienced extracurricular activities, and offer explanations of why the particular patterns of participation were found.

Degree of Participation

The first question we addressed dealt with the frequency of participation in extracurricular activities. Given the difficulties of communicating with hearing participants and of transportation home after school, it was possible that very few students in the longitudinal study participated in extracurricular activities. On the other hand, if a relatively large portion of the students participated, this would suggest that the various barriers could be dealt with effectively enough to permit taking part in activities. On the basis of the students' responses to questions on the Social Activity Scale they were divided into three groups with respect to degree of participation in extracurricular activities. Figure 6.1 shows the proportion in each of the three groups and the types of activities in which those who were involved participated. About one-fourth of the students participated in no extracurriculars during their four years of high school. Roughly half participated in at least one activity during their four years and up to one activity annually. The remaining quarter of the students participated in at least one activity on an annual basis and sometimes in more than one activity.

These results suggest that there was fairly widespread participation in extracurriculars among the deaf students, but we do not have data to determine whether extent of participation by this group was comparable to that of their hearing schoolmates. Holcomb's (1990) study, which included groups of deaf and hearing subjects, asked about participation in various extracurricular activities. He found that, for these groups of first year college students who were recalling their high school experiences, level of participation was fairly comparable for the two groups, although the hearing students participated somewhat more in a few activities.

The extent of involvement by the deaf students in the longitudinal study suggests that barriers to participation were regularly overcome, and speaks to the efforts of schools in providing communication and transportation support to students so that participation was possible. The extent of participation may also reflect the students' high motivation, resilience in the face of difficulties, and their determination to succeed (Stewart & Stinson, 1992).

We should also note that these data do not provide any information regarding the quality of the experience; whether students felt they were

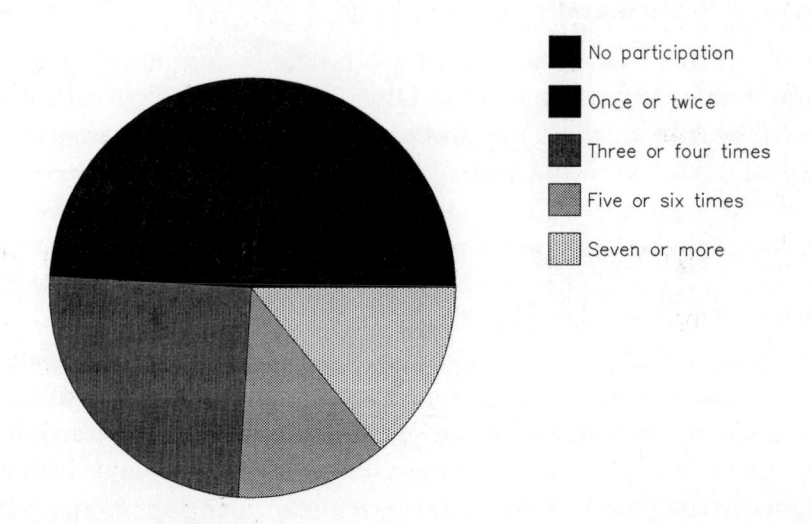

Figure 6.1
Frequency of Participation Over Four Years

- No participation
- Once or twice
- Three or four times
- Five or six times
- Seven or more

involved as full, active members, or as marginal, passive members who were not really enjoying the experience.

Types of Activities

The next issue we addressed concerned the types of activities in which students participated. One question was whether students participated in any activities that might enhance their pride in being deaf and in learning about the Deaf community and Deaf culture. Another question was whether students tended to focus their participation into certain types of activities. For example, was athletics a "natural" kind of activity that would attract many deaf participants because performance would generally not depend as much on verbal skills as would other activities such as student government? The right half of figure 6.2 provides information pertinent to these questions. This part of the figure shows that for those students who reported participating in at least one extracurricular activity during high school, the most frequently selected categories were sports, either intramural or extramural, or the category called "other." This "other" category included the activities of the Junior National Association for the Deaf, other specifically deafness oriented activities, jazz band, drill team, dance clubs, and pep club. Since many of the activities in this "other" category were specifically deafness oriented, these results indicate that schools are making some effort to provide activities that foster links to the Deaf community.

The single largest category of extracurricular activities was in fact intramural sports, with all sports representing the most common category of activity. A surprising number of students were involved in drama events. Deaf students were much less likely to be involved in the school paper, honor society, or student government. Before one sees a conspiracy here (i.e. concludes that deaf students were systematically excluded from certain activities where there is widespread participation by hearing schoolmates), we should put these numbers in perspective. In most high schools the largest coordinated extracurricular effort is for varsity and intramural sports. A simple test of this assertion is to count the number of faces in the school yearbook by activity. Sports teams and activities that support sports take up a considerable amount of space in the yearbook. School government, publications, and the honor society are relatively small activities in relation to the total number of students in school. What Figure 6.2 reflects is a general pattern of school participation not unlike that we would find among hearing students in most high schools.

This point is borne out by comparison of our findings with those of Holcomb's (1990). He found that there was a heavy selection of athletic activities by both hearing and deaf students. Varsity sports was the most frequently selected activity by both groups of students and intramural sports was the second most frequently selected category for both groups in Holcomb's study. "Social clubs" seemed to include the types of activities that were placed in the "other" category, which was another one of the most frequently selected categories by our subjects. Student government and student newspaper, unpopular activities among our students were also relatively less popular activities in the Holcomb study even though these were students who subsequently attended college. Two of the activities in which few of our students participated, "honor society" and "student government," were activities for which Holcomb found significantly less involvement among the deaf students than among the hearing ones. These activities appear to be ones where verbal proficiency may have been important.

An additional analysis was performed to determine whether the patterns of participation for those who were involved in several activities during the high school years was different than the patterns of participation for those who had participated in at least one activity. The frequency of participation in different activities for students who were involved in several activities is presented in Figure 6.2.

An examination of the Figure shows that for students who were involved in several activities, the contribution of the "other" category declines. Comparison of the figures also shows that those who were more frequent participants were more likely to be involved in verbal activities such as school publications and drama. The change in the frequency of participation in the "other" category suggests that those who participated in only one activity or fewer each year were more likely to join an activity that had a deafness focus, such as the Junior National Association of the Deaf, or specialty activity, such as a drill team. Those who participated in multiple activities each year may have participated repeatedly in one type of activity, such as sports or drama; *or* these active participants could have distributed participation among various activities, both sport and non-sport.

These active participants appeared less likely to join activities in the "other" category.

Figure 6.2
Participation in Extra-Curriculars

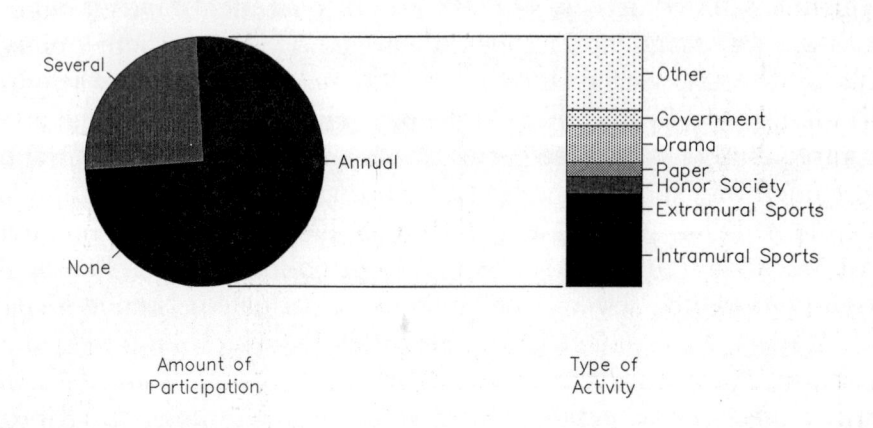

Predicting Participation

We had two questions that were related to predicting the extent of involvement in extracurriculars: "What were the differences between students who participated in many activities and those who participated in few," and "What program factors were related to extent of participation?" Among the characteristics of students that might be related to extent of participation were gender, family resources, and communication preference and skills. With respect to gender, males may participate more actively in extracurriculars than females because sports are the most widely available activities and males tend to participate in them more than females. Students with greater family resources might be more likely to participate because the family can provide various kinds of supports that make participation easier and parents with greater resources may be more likely to encourage their children to participate. Possible relations between communication skill and preference and participation are not so straightforward. On one hand, it could be argued that students with better speech skills can more easily communicate with hearing schoolmates and would be more comfortable in extracurricular activities with such peers. On the other hand, such oral students may avoid activities with a specific deafness orientation that students with weaker speech skills might be more likely to join. Furthermore, a student with weaker speech skills may be likely to join other deaf students and participate in an extracurricular activity together with the support of an interpreter, and such deaf students who can participate as a group may, in fact, be among the most frequent deaf participants. Two program factors that would be expected to be associated with greater participation would be the provision of transportation home after school and the provision of interpreters for extracurricular activities.

In identifying factors that predicted extent of involvement, we used that same general model employed for generating the other path analyses that are reported in this book. A model with the variables that had statistically significant paths to extracurricular participation is shown in Figure 6.3. There were three variables that contributed to the prediction of participation: Access to after school transportation (beta = .100, $p < .02$); student's gender (beta = $-.129$, $p < .004$); family resources (beta = $-.115$, $p < .04$). These variables accounted for 11.4% of the variance in extracurricular participation.

In general, males tended to participate in extracurriculars more frequently than did females. Males on the average participated in some kind of extracurricular activity each year of their four years in high school while females participated in only three of their four years. However, the variance for males was greater than for females which suggests that a smaller number of males participated in more extracurriculars.

Figure 6.3
Predicting Extra-curricular Participation

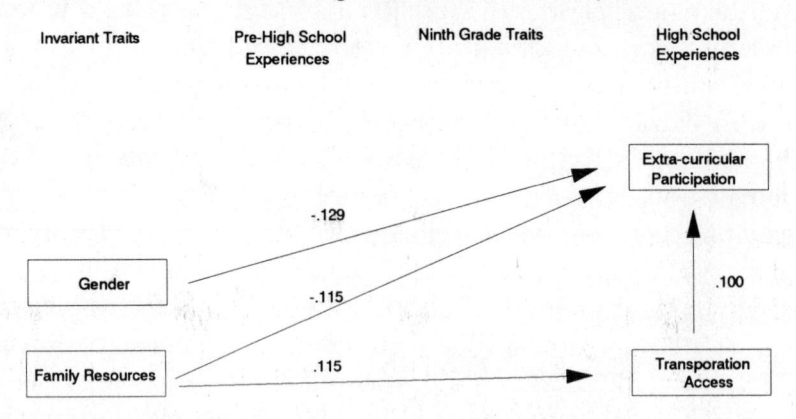

| Invariant Traits | Pre-High School Experiences | Ninth Grade Traits | High School Experiences |

- Gender → Extra-curricular Participation: -.129
- Gender → Transportation Access: -.115
- Family Resources → Extra-curricular Participation: -.115
- Family Resources → Transportation Access: .115
- Transportation Access → Extra-curricular Participation: .100

To further examine the relationship between gender and participation in extracurriculars, Figure 6.4 was generated which shows the percent of males and females participating in different numbers of activities in a year. A consideration of Figure 6.4 indicates two things about girls' participation. First, a large percentage of girls simply did not participate in any activity. Second, at and beyond an average of two or more activities per year, males were more likely to be represented than females. A simple interpretation of these results is that sports are the most widely available high school extracurricular and that they tend to draw more boys than girls, therefore greater participation among boys is not surprising.

However, this interpretation needs to be qualified by a consideration of differences between single-activity and multiple-activity participant's choices. These considerations will be addressed below. Basically, the more activities one is in, the more likely some of those activities are going to be sports. Males participate in organized sports at a higher rate than females. Hence, the contribution of gender to the path analysis involves several related considerations.

Students who had some sort of after school transportation solution participated in 50% more activities than those who did not. The distributions of the two groups was not equal. There was considerably more variance in participation for the students who had no transportation solution. In other words, some of those adolescents participated in a number of activities. What this suggests is that there is a threshold or gate in relation to transportation. Some individuals will participate regardless of the challenge of transportation; however, for most students

Figure 6.4
Comparison of Male and Female
Extra—curricular Participation

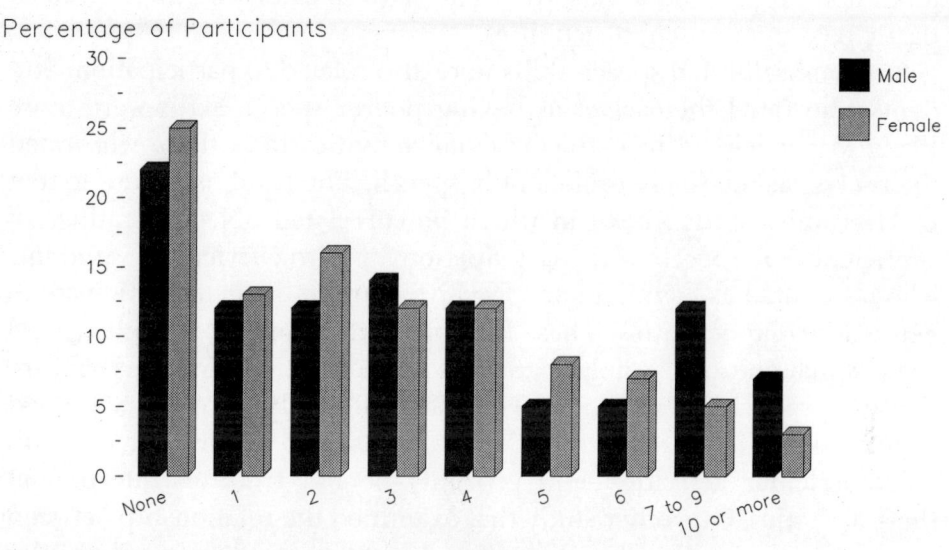

the absence of a good after-school transportation solution will mean that they do not participate or must sharply curtail their degree of participation.

Students with more family resources were more likely to participate in extracurriculars than were those who had fewer family resources. This relationship, however, was qualified by the extent the student participated in extracurricular activities. For individuals who participated in one activity per year—a group we will discuss below as tending to specialize in a single kind of activity—family resources had no impact on their participation; however, for individuals who participated in three or more activities per year, family resources were a major factor. Probably without family financial support, help with school work, and transportation alternatives these children could not have been as fully involved as they were. What is interesting to note is that this picture of the deaf student very involved in extracurriculars begins to look like the typical suburban adolescent who is heavily involved in school activities. "Behind every successful class president is a pushy mom."

Additional evidence of the significant role of family resources is provided by the significant path from family resources to transportation. Family resources predicted 1.3 percent of the variance in access to after school transportation (beta = .115; p = .008). Rides are essential for participating in after school activities, and for many students these rides must come from parents. Essentially, more affluent parents were slightly more able to provide a variety of alternatives to enable their child to participate in after-school activities.

Students' self-rated speech skills were also related to participation. Students who rated themselves as having poorer speech skills were more likely to participate in extracurricular activities than those who rated themselves as relatively proficient in speech. The result is similar to that of Holcomb's study (1990) in which he correlated objective ratings of proficiency in speech with participation in extracurriculars. Students who were rated as having poor speech were more likely to participate in extracurricular activities. These findings and those of Holcomb's (1990) suggest that one group of deaf students in mainstream programs who are likely to participate are those who have relatively poor speech, good signing skills, have a group of deaf students with whom they can join extracurricular activities, and probably benefit from an interpret at these activities. One other study that examined the relationship between communication skill and participation in extracurriculars found no relationship between communication preference and participation (Stewart & Stinson, 1992). Thus, no study found that students with better oral skills were more likely to participate in extracurriculars, and there is no support for the idea that good oral skills are necessary for participation in such activities.

This lack of an overall relationship does not, of course, preclude the possibility that there is another group of deaf students who often participate in extracurriculars who tend to rely on their oral skills, do not use an interpreter, and generally participate in activities with few or no other deaf participants.

Another interpretation of the association between poor speech skill and participation in extracurriculars is that the students with good speech skills are able to readily involve themselves in informal activities with hearing peers, and thus they participate less in extracurricular activities because they do not need them for friendship and social support.

Two other relationships in the model shown in Figure 6.3 should be noted. Degree of mainstreaming has a slight negative correlation with the deaf student's degree of extracurricular participation during his or her four years in a local public high school ($r = -.105$; $p < .02$). We have a question of statistical significance and practical insignificance in this correlation. While the relationship is statistically significant, it accounts for only 1% of the variance between the two factors; thus we might reasonably conclude that the relationship is for practical purposes non-existent. In addition, less than 1% of the variance in speech skill was predicted by gender (beta = .088; p < .04).

Type of Participation

A final question we addressed was why did some students participate in athletics; why did others participate in non-athletic activities; and why did others participate in a combination of the two? Based on their interests in extra-curriculars, four groups of students could be identified: non-participants (23.2%), non-athletic types (29.3%), athletic only (13.8%), and varied activity participants (33.7%). The non-athletic types participated in drama, newspaper, and other types of extra-curriculars without being active in either intramural or varsity sports. The athletic types participated in either intramural or varsity sports, but in no other types of extra-curriculars.

We computed a discriminant analysis to differentiate among the four groups of students. We used the variables from the path analysis that predicted degree of participation in extracurriculars (speech skill, access to after-school transportation, family resource, and gender) and the invariant traits not included in the path analysis (signing skill, race, and degree of hearing loss). The discriminant analysis produced three functions in order to differentiate among the groups. The first function consisted of the student's self-rated signing ability, access to afterschool transportation, family resources, and race. The second function only included gender. The third function was a measure of English communication in that included the degree of the student's hearing loss and the student's self-rated speech skills.

The first function differentiated the non-participants from the rest of the students and those who participated in non-athletics from the non-participants. The non-participants had poorer signing skills, had less access to after school transportation, had less affluent families, and were more likely to be members of minority groups. Those who participated in non-athletic activities, and this includes those who participated in both athletic and non-athletics, had better signing skills, had more access to after school transportation, had more affluent families, and were more likely to be white.

The second discriminant function which included only gender differentiated between those who participated in athletics and those who did not. Basically males were more likely to be participants in athletics and females were more likely to participate in non-athletic extracurriculars.

The third function did not contribute significantly to the analysis; however, it should be noted that better speech skills differentiated between students who participated only in athletics and those who participated in athletics and other extra-curriculars.

The typical non-participant is a minority group member or a child from a less affluent family who has little access to extra-curricular programs after school. The modal non-athletic extra-curricular participant is a female from an affluent family with good access to after school activities. The modal athletics only participant is a male with weaker speech skills. The individual who participates in several activities, both athletic and non-athletic, is a male from an affluent family who has more access to after school transportation and has better speech skills.

SUMMARY

It is desirable that educational programs for deaf students in public schools take into account participation in extracurricular activities as part of their overall educational experience. Extracurricular activities contribute to the transmission of the cultural values and norms of society and to the impartation of the skills necessary for becoming a competent adult (Holland & Andre, 1987; Stewart & Stinson, 1992). This view of extracurricular activities is part of the perspective that emphasizes the whole student, not just academic achievement; and in the case of the deaf student, this view means not just American Sign Language, written English, and/or spoken English. An important benefit of extracurricular activities for deaf students in public school that is unique for them is enculturation into Deaf culture and the Deaf community (Janesick & Moores, 1992; Stewart & Stinson, 1992).

It also may be fairly easy for deaf students in public schools to have unrewarding experiences in extracurricular activities if they do not receive special support and attention. The particular type of support desirable for these students is probably not uniform and depends on the particular needs of the individual deaf participant.

Results from the longitudinal study suggest that there was a reasonably widespread level of participation among the deaf students in these public school programs. In numerous cases, this extent of participation speaks to the students' motivation, resilience, and ability to cope with barriers such as communication with hearing school mates. We do not know much about the quality of students' experiences in extracurriculars. According to the arguments of critics of mainstreaming such as Garretson (in Jacobs, 1989) and Lane (1992), deaf students in such activities are likely to have very passive experiences and it is virtually impossible for them to have positions of leadership. Holcomb's (1990) study also suggests that deaf students have fewer leadership opportunities than do their hearing counterparts. It is easy to think of circumstances where these kinds of things can happen. But it appears that public school programs also regularly offer experiences where leadership and active participation are quite likely to occur for the deaf students, such as in sign choir, open to both deaf and hearing participants, but with most of them being deaf. We would also like to learn more about the comfort levels of the deaf participants in extracurricular activities. Under what conditions was the experience of participation most rewarding, and under what conditions was it least rewarding?

Chapter 7

DEVELOPMENT OF SOCIAL COMPETENCE

In fostering the social development of deaf students, what particular behaviors, cognitive processes, and affective states should be of concern to educators? One important idea is that the individual has the attributes, skills, and resources to obtain what he or she wants in various social situations (Wrubel, Benner & Lazarus, 1981). This set of capacities has been referred to as social competence. Greenberg (1983) described social competence as a broad construct that includes the characteristics of (a) thinking independently, (b) being able to direct oneself, (c) flexibility in being able to adapt to the needs of diverse situations, and (d) ability to rely upon others and to be relied upon by others.

It seems desirable to foster the development of competencies that will enable students to exercise control over their social affairs, as is appropriate for the situation. Given the frequent communication difficulties experienced by deaf people and the limited understanding of the special subcultural status of deaf people in society, development of social competence is a formidable challenge for educators of deaf students (Greenberg & Kusche, 1989; Stinson, in press).

There are two broad sets of relationships that each student must deal with and handle effectively if he or she is to be socially competent at school: (a) relationships with teachers and other school personnel, and (b) relationships with peers. Hatch (1987) noted the importance of student-teacher relations: "Teacher-to-child interaction may be the primary vehicle through which children learn the complex social lessons required for successful performance in academic institutions (p. 176)." Positive relationships with peers are also important for healthy functioning in school and provide an additional basis for learning to participate in society and for developing good psychological health (Johnson, 1980). In our study we examined the quality of these relationships as viewed by the students themselves.

SOCIAL MATURITY AT SCHOOL

Social maturity within a school setting refers to those behaviors that are associated with performing competently, functioning independently, relating well to others, and acting responsibly (Meadow, 1980; 1983a). The measure of social maturity developed by Meadow (1983a) for school settings, and used in our study, involves teacher's ratings of the extent that students exhibited positive classroom and school behaviors, and not just "problem" and "pathological" behaviors. It should be realized that the measure is sensitive to the impressions the child makes on the teachers, as well as to the teacher's experiences in interacting with and instructing the child. Thus, while ratings of social maturity are likely to reflect the child's actual ability and emotional resources for adapting to and functioning well in the classroom setting, they can also reflect teacher's strain from difficulty in communicating with and instructing the child, or the lack of such strain (Furth, 1973; Lane, 1989; Stinson, in press). Students who are easy to teach, make favorable impressions upon others, and thus tend to elicit favorable feedback in the educational environment, are likely to be assessed as having high social maturity (Kluwin & Sweet, 1990).

The measure of social maturity we used, *The Social-Emotional Assessment Inventory,* (Meadow, 1983a) has three dimensions: (a) Items tapping *social adjustment* pertain to the demonstration of positive social behaviors such as following rules and cooperating as opposed to misbehaving, being aggressive, teasing, and not following rules. (b) Items measuring *self image* deal with self confidence, effort in communicating with others, motivation to learn and related matters. (c) Those tapping *emotional adjustment* pertain to being calm, realistic, and balanced, as opposed to being fearfully, anxious and having negative feelings about one's motor skills (Meadow, 1983a; Meadow, 1983b). The total score, then, includes these three dimensions. One characteristic that has been linked with social competence, and with social maturity in particular, for both deaf and hearing children and youths, has been communication skill (Greenberg, 1983; Hatch, 1987). Good communication skills are necessary for understanding self and others, planning and engaging in social interactions, and in interpreting the feedback that occurs during interaction (Greenberg, 1983). For example, just one aspect of these communication skills is the vocabulary necessary for self analysis of internal events that includes cognitive words such as, "sad," "happy," "excited," and "frustrated" (Meadow, 1980). This vocabulary is important for sensitive analysis of how one's self is thinking and feeling in the social situation, for sharing thoughts and feelings with others, and for accurately interpreting the actions and comments of others (Greenberg & Kusche, 1989). The relationship between communicative competence and social maturity has been demonstrated empirically. For example, deaf preschool children rated high in communicative competence have been found to show higher social maturity than those rated low in communicative competence (Schlesinger & Meadow, 1971). As Greenberg (1983, p. 8) noted, "Deafness, itself, does not lead to poor social competence: poor and limited communication leads to poor social competence."

An additional factor related to the social maturity of deaf students is home environment (Greenberg & Kusche, 1989; Meadow, 1980). For example, for deaf children with hearing parents, relatively frequent contact with parents appears to promote social maturity. Quarrington and Solomon (1975) found that for deaf students attending a residential school, more frequent visits home were associated with greater social maturity.

PREDICTING SOCIAL MATURITY IN THE 12TH GRADE

The model of educational processes and outcomes we have advanced suggests that social maturity may be influenced by invariant traits, pre-high school experiences, ninth grade traits and high school experiences. As noted, one trait that may predict social maturity is communicative competence. Whether or not a relationship is obtained may depend partly on the measures used. In the present study, the measures of communication skill were self-ratings of proficiency in speech and sign. It is not altogether clear how closely such student ratings would be associated with teacher's ratings of student's classroom behavior. Another factor that may predict social maturity is extent of mainstreaming into regular classes, as opposed to placement in special classes. In a review of studies on mainstreaming, Davis (1986) noted that personality factors (in a broad sense that would include social maturity) contribute to performance in mainstreamed classes. Academic skills may also be related to social maturity. Students who do well academically are likely to show characteristics such as high self-esteem and motivation to learn (Skinner, Wellborne & Connell, 1990; Stinson, in press; Wentzel, 1991). These characteristics were among those tapped by items comprising the measure of social maturity.

Because social maturity at the end of high school could be substantially affected by social maturity at the start of high school and thus obscure factors that would influence maturity development during high school, ninth grade social maturity was regressed against twelfth grade social maturity. The resulting adjusted twelfth grade social maturity score was then used in a path analysis as the dependent variable. This analysis showed that four variables predicted social maturity in the twelfth grade. As is shown in Figure 7.1, there were significant paths from ninth grade social maturity (beta = .340 $p < .001$), from ninth grade achievement (beta = .241, $p < .001$), high school placement (beta = .147, $p < .02$), and from academic track (beta = .115, $p < .04$) to twelfth grade social maturity. Ninth grade social maturity accounted for 12% of the variance in adjusted twelfth grade social maturity, and the other three variables, achievement, placement, and track, accounted for an additional 18% of the variance.

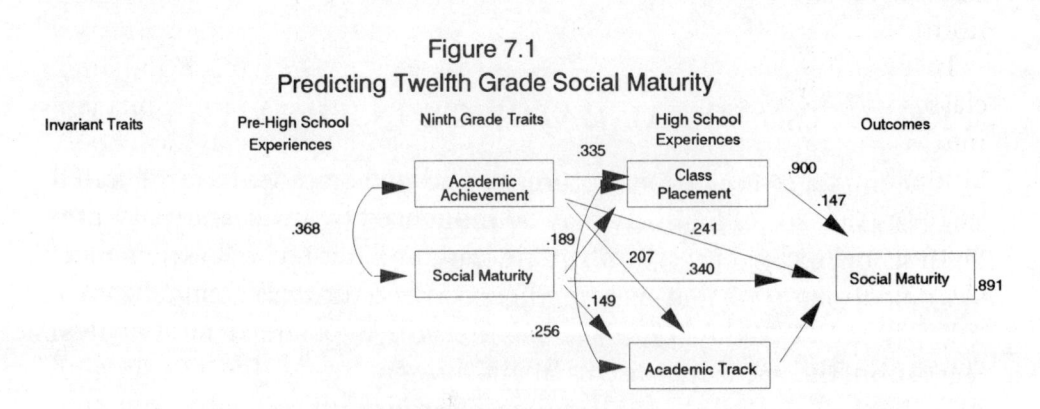

Figure 7.1
Predicting Twelfth Grade Social Maturity

Students with higher levels of achievement in the ninth grade were perceived by teachers in the twelfth grade as showing greater social maturity. Students who demonstrated greater academic achievement may have received high ratings for social maturity in part because some of the characteristics of social maturity are behaviors that facilitate classroom learning. These behaviors include working hard, paying attention, doing assignments, studying lessons, and participating in a positive way in group activities (Wentzel, 1991). It is also possible that teachers' knowledge of their students' previous academic achievement influenced ratings. Teachers may have tended to assign higher ratings of social maturity to students they knew were doing well academically.

An underlying factor in the relationship between academic achievement and social maturity may have been the communication skills of the student. Good communication skills have been associated with social maturity because such skills help one select and execute the kinds of social interactions that make favorable impressions on others (Greenberg, 1983; Greenberg & Kusche, 1989). The measure of academic achievement may have in part reflected communication skill, as students with greater proficiency in English are likely to do better on tests of academic performance.

Self-ratings of proficiency in speech or in sign were not, however, related to social maturity. It is quite possible that these self-rated communication skills are somewhat different from those relevant to the teacher-rated measure of social maturity. For students, the basis of these self-ratings may have been such factors as ability to produce speech or sign and judgements of the extent that others can comprehend their productions. Such self-ratings may have little to do with the strategic and analytic communication skills that are also necessary for effective social interaction and that may be more likely to influence ratings of social maturity.

In addition, extent of placement into an academic track and into classes with hearing peers were related to social maturity. Students fell into two groups on the basis of their academic track in high school. Students in general and academic tracks were considered to be more socially mature than students in vocational tracks. High school placement formed four distinct groups. Students who were kept in separate classes had the lowest adjusted twelfth grade social maturity. Students who had periodically or regularly been mainstreamed into an academic class had higher twelfth grade ratings of social maturity. Students who were mainstreamed for at least one academic class on a regular basis and sometimes for several academic classes had the next highest adjusted score. The highest scores were seen among students who were consistently mainstreamed for two or more classes.

Note in Figure 7.1, that there are also significant paths from ninth grade social maturity to extent of mainstreaming and to the type of academic track into which the student is placed. Thus, initial social maturity appears to influence the kinds of academic high school experiences the student has. Explicitly or implicitly, social maturity may have been among the characteristics used to place students into academically oriented tracks and mainstreamed classes. These educational experiences, in turn, may affect subsequent social maturity. Students placed in these settings appear to maintain their high level of social maturity. Certain qualities of these educational settings, such as high expectations and encouragement of independence, in conjunction with the personality characteristics and abilities students bring to the setting may foster social maturity (Kluwin, 1992).

We now turn to considering the second component of social competence addressed in the study, relationships with peers.

ORIENTATIONS TO DEAF AND HEARING PEERS

Deaf students tend to perceive their relationships with other deaf peers more positively than those with hearing ones (Foster, 1989; Stinson & Whitmire, 1991). The obvious barrier to deaf-hearing relationships is communication, especially if the deaf student relies primarily on sign language. Meadow (1980) also found that relationships across peer groups may be impeded by negative attitudes which are sometimes held by hearing adolescents toward deaf peers. At the same time, a frequent goal of mainstream programs has been the fostering of positive relationships between deaf and hearing peers. Thus, it is desirable to include consideration of orientations toward both deaf and hearing peers in a study of the social development of deaf adolescents in public school settings.

What dimensions should be included in a measure of social orientation? The measure we used combines the dimensions of participation and relatedness. Participation includes verbal and non-verbal communication between peers and the inclusion of the student in in-class and out-of-class activities with peers (Antia, 1985; Kaufman, Gottlieb, Agard & Kukic, 1975). As used here, participation refers to self-reports of the level of involvement in three areas: (a) class (e.g. helping other students), (b) school (e.g. eating lunch with friends), and (c) outside-of-school activities (e.g. visiting a friend's house).

The second dimension in social orientation is relatedness (Connell, 1990). Relatedness pertains to the extent that one is accepted and approved of by his or her peers (Antia, 1985). Such acceptance is the most valued indicator of social integration with one's peers. Following a motivational framework proposed by Connell (1990), relatedness refers to self-appraisals of the emotional security of one's relationships with significant others. Emotional security is a perception of positive stability in relationships, such as reporting that one feels "happy" and "relaxed" in relationships with peers. Relatedness may be closely associated with the extent to which individuals identify with particular social groups and feel relational bonds with individuals within them. Ainsworth (1989) has characterized such bonds as reflecting relationships that are close, enduring and affectionate. There are feelings of cooperation, reciprocity and trust that permit friends to reveal their feelings to each other and feel that there is mutual understanding.

Orientation to Deaf Peers

As noted, deaf students are generally more emotionally secure and feel more accepted in relationships with deaf peers than in those with hearing peers. This is generally true regardless of whether the student is in a residential (or separate day) school, or in a public school program, either large or small (Stinson, Chase & Kluwin, 1990; Stinson & Whitmire, 1992; Stinson, Siple, Chase & Bondi-Wolcott; 1990). While these general trends should be kept in mind, it is also important to recognize that the extent of orientation to deaf peers varies substantially among the deaf and hard of hearing students enrolled in public school programs.

Orientation to Hearing Peers

The extent of deaf students' social orientation to hearing peers may also be influenced by a variety of factors including extent of contact with hearing peers, situational difficulties, support of others, and personal capabilities. For example, students who are frequently placed in classes with hearing peers may not be able to adequately understand the teacher and classroom discussion (Foster, 1988; Saur, Lane, Hurley & Opton, 1986). Perceptions regarding participation may also reflect the extent to which students think that peers and adults are supportive and cooperative. For example, deaf students may attribute their lack of participation in social activities to the unwillingness of hearing schoolmates to maintain conversations beyond superficialities, to extend invitations to parties, etc. (Foster, 1988). Finally the extent of participation may depend on personal qualities of the student, such as preparation for class, willingness to contribute to class discussion, friendliness, and outgoingness. Deaf students have stated that limited participation is a major concern in the mainstream setting (Foster, 1988; Saur et al., 1986).

Interest in friendship with hearing peers varies considerably among deaf adolescents. Many deaf students interact considerably with hearing peers, including in unstructured, out-of-class situations. For example, deaf adolescents enrolled in public school programs are about equally likely to report participation in outside of school activities, such as visiting a friend's house or going to a movie, with hearing as with deaf peers (Stinson, Chase & Kluwin, 1990). At the same time, minimal interaction in the classroom between deaf and hearing peers has been noted as we pointed out in Chapter 6.

Independence of Orientations to Deaf and Hearing Peers

It is possible for students who have strong social orientations toward deaf peers to have either *strong* or *weak* orientations toward hearing peers. Glickman (1986) describes four possible social orientation patterns of deaf youths: (a) Is socially oriented toward deaf peers and has a critical view of interactions with hearing peers; (b) is socially oriented toward hearing peers and shows little interest in interactions with deaf peers; (c) has positive social orientations toward both deaf and hearing peers; (d) those who do not have positive social orientations, or feel at home with either group. Data from students enrolled in public school programs suggest that their social orientations are distributed over these four alternatives rather than in one particular alternative (Stinson, et. al., 1990; see also Chapter 5). In our analysis, degree of social orientation toward hearing peers did not significantly correlate with degree of orientation toward deaf peers. Thus, students who are favorably oriented toward deaf peers may be favorably or unfavorably oriented toward hearing ones. In addition, as noted earlier, when we factor analyzed eight scales referring to participation and relatedness with either deaf or hearing peers, the scales loaded onto two separate factors on the basis of whether items referred to relationships with hearing or deaf peers. All of these considerations point to the importance of independently identifying predictors of orientation to hearing peers and of orientation to deaf peers.

PREDICTING ORIENTATION TO DEAF PEERS IN THE TWELFTH GRADE

Communication skill is a personal trait that may be associated with orientation toward deaf peers in the public school setting. Students with greater proficiency in sign language may have stronger orientations to deaf peers than those with less proficiency. In addition, a high school

Figure 7.2
Predicting Orientation to Deaf Peers

| Invariant Traits | Pre-High School Experiences | Ninth Grade Traits | High School Experiences | Outcomes |

Hearing Loss → .253 → Orientation to Deaf Peers (.862)

Hearing Loss → .185 → Signing Skill (.984) → .311 → Orientation to Deaf Peers

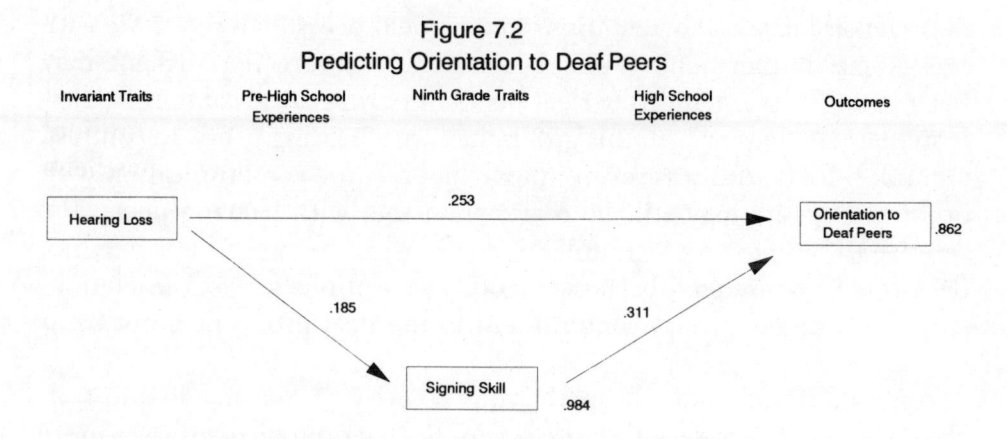

experience that may be related to orientation is the extent that the student is in special classes with other deaf peers (as opposed to being mainstreamed into classes with hearing peers). Students spending relatively more time in special classes presumably interact more with deaf peers and less with hearing peers and, consequently, may develop stronger social orientations toward deaf classmates.

What variables predicted orientation to deaf peers? Figure 7.2 shows a model with variables that significantly predict orientation to deaf peers, and it is apparent that communication skills are the dimensions that are associated with this orientation. There are statistically significant paths from a perceived signing skill to orientation to deaf peers (beta = .311; $p < .001$) and from the degree of hearing loss to orientation (beta = .253; $p < .001$). The equation represented by this model accounted for 26% of the variance in orientation to deaf peers.

Students who rated themselves as skilled in sign language were more likely to be oriented toward deaf peers than those who rated themselves as less skilled. These results are consistent with those of Stinson and his associates (1989) who reported that deaf students who preferred American Sign Language or total communication reported more frequent interaction and closer relationships with other deaf peers than did those who preferred oral communication. Individuals who are comfortable with sign language may feel a closer bond to deaf people as a social group because shared ways of communicating are basic to formation of social relationships and to access to social networks, and because development of sign skills goes hand in hand with personal commitment to the group (Heller, 1987).

In addition students who had more severe hearing impairment reported more favorable social orientations toward deaf peers than did those with less severe impairment. Students with more severe impairment may have stronger orientations to deaf peers in part because communication is substantially easier with this group than with hearing peers. In contrast, for individuals with less severe impairment, while communication with other deaf peers may still be easier than that with hearing peers, the relative difference in communication ease with the two groups may not be as great; consequently, because of more options for social relationships with either group, commitment to the deaf group may not be as strong.

Another finding was the path from severity of hearing loss to self-rated sign skill. Those with more severe hearing impairment were more likely to rate themselves as high in sign proficiency. This result is not surprising since this group is more dependent on visual means for communication.

It is interesting that the extent of placement in special classes did not predict orientation to deaf peers, although we originally considered it a likely predictor. How can the failure of placement to predict be explained? A possible answer is that deaf students in these programs had at least some meaningful contact with deaf peers, regardless of the extent they were mainstreamed, and that it was sufficient for a positive social orientation to deaf peers to emerge. In other words, the strong bonds with the deaf group appeared to have a greater impact on the establishment and maintenance of social relationships than the extent of time in mainstream or deaf classes. The deaf peer group was important for support, friendship, and relaxed communication. The tendency of students with an orientation to deaf peers to be good signers and to have a more severe hearing loss was similar to findings in Chapter 5 for the group of students who reported having a relatively large number of deaf friends, but few hearing friends. This group of students also tended to be good signers and to rate themselves as having poor speech, which is associated with more severe hearing loss. Taken together these results show how the social relationships of students depends on their communication skills.

Predicting 12th Grade Orientation to Hearing Peers

Communication skill and preference may predict degree of social orientation to hearing peers, just as it predicts orientation to deaf peers. In this case, however, the variation is in oral skill, because proficiency in oral communication should facilitate interaction with hearing peers. In addition, the extent that the student is placed in mainstream classes with hearing peers may be related to orientation toward hearing classmates. With increased mainstreaming, participation of deaf students in activities with hearing peers might increase because physical placement generates more contact and opportunities.

A path-analytic model was developed in which four factors predicted orientation to hearing peers, and this model is shown in Figure 7.3. There were significant paths to orientation toward hearing peers from degree of hearing loss (beta = $-.228$; $p < .001$), perceived signing skill (beta = $-.144$; $p < .01$), gender (beta = $-.134$, $p < .025$), and degree of mainstream class placement during high school (beta = $.152$; $p < .025$). This model accounts for 19% of the variance in orientation to hearing peers.

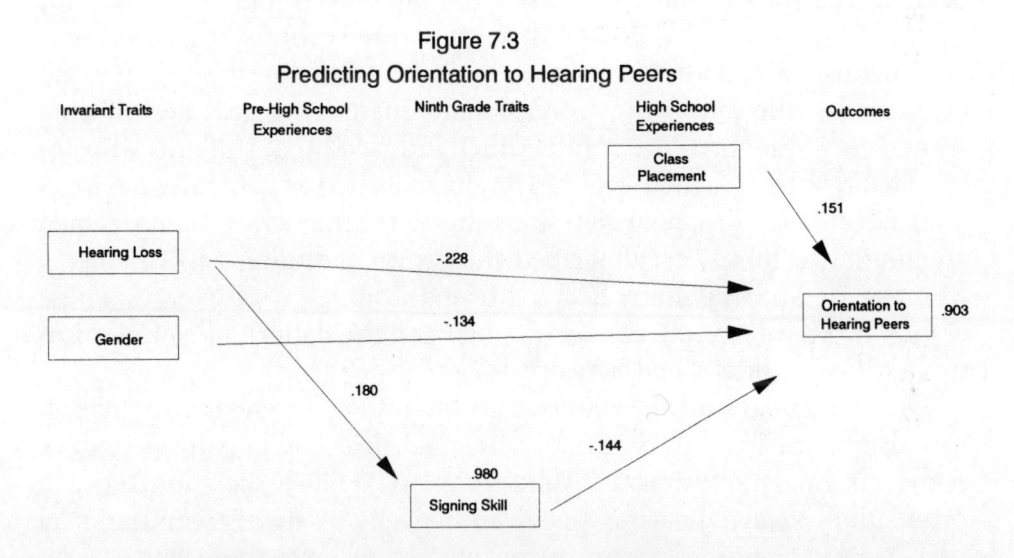

Figure 7.3
Predicting Orientation to Hearing Peers

These results show that students with moderate hearing impairment are more likely to have a favorable orientation to hearing peers than those with more severe impairment. In addition, students who perceived themselves as relatively weak in sign proficiency had stronger social orientations to hearing peers than those who considered themselves proficient in sign language. Although this is a gross generalization (and we personally know of exceptions to it), those who considered themselves relatively weak in sign may have had comparatively good oral skills. The significant path indicating that students with relatively moderate hearing loss tended to rate themselves as relatively poor signers supports the inferred relationship between weak signing skill and oral proficiency. Students with relatively moderate hearing loss are likely to have better oral skills (Sims, Walter & Whitehead, 1982). Taken together, these results and reasoning suggest that those students who had relatively good oral skills and who felt comfortable about using them may have been more likely to experience positive social relationships with hearing peers than those who had poor skills and who felt uncomfortable using them. Consistent with this interpretation, Davis (1986) in reviewing research on effects of mainstreaming suggests that oral communication skills may be associated with successful adjustment, without specifying whether it is academic or social.

An additional finding was that students more frequently mainstreamed into classes with hearing peers had more positive social orientations to hearing classmates than did those less frequently mainstreamed, with extent of mainstreaming broken down into three groups: Students regularly mainstreamed for two or more subjects had the most positive social orientation, followed by those occasionally mainstreamed, and full-time special class students. The results which indicated that students who are oriented toward hearing peers can be characterized as generally having a moderate hearing loss, poor sign skills, and being frequently mainstreamed are similar to those that described the group of students in Chapter 5 who reported having many hearing friends, but few deaf friends. These results also reinforce the connection between the pattern of communication skills and one's social network.

This same relationship between mainstreaming and social orientation was also found in a study of mainstreamed deaf students in secondary schools in England (Stinson & Whitmire, 1991). The association between orientation toward hearing peers and extent of mainstreaming may reflect (a) changes in opportunity for interaction, since those who experience more mainstreaming spend more time with hearing classmates and less time with deaf peers; and (b) differences in characteristics of students, since those who are frequently mainstreamed may have better oral skills, academic skills, and so on (Davis, 1986). It is not clear, however, whether the stronger orientation toward hearing peers as a function of mainstreaming reflected perceptions of greater participation in activities with hearing peers on a relatively superficial level or establishment of deeper relationships of acceptance and trust.

The results also revealed that boys were more likely to be oriented toward hearing peers than were girls. Some possible reasons for this relationship are that, for our sample, boys had better speech skills and were more frequently mainstreamed than girls. These factors are likely to facilitate orientation to hearing peers. An additional possibility as noted in Chapter 6 is that boys participate more in extra-curriculars than girls which would provide them with more structured experiences with hearing peers as noted by Stinson and Whitmire (1990) to be contributory to more frequent and positive interactions.

SUMMARY

Social orientations toward deaf and toward hearing peers were also related to school experiences and student characteristics. The modal graduating deaf student who is positively oriented toward his hearing peers is a male with a relatively moderate hearing loss, has been in many mainstream classes in high school, and does not perceive himself as a good signer. The typical student who is oriented toward deaf peers perceives him or herself as a skilled signer and has a profound hearing loss.

Both student characteristics and educational experience are factors in the social development of deaf students in the public schools. Social maturity was related to academic achievement and educational placement, perhaps in a cyclical manner. The connection of social maturity with academic achievement is also true for hearing students, and is consistent with the conclusion that learning and behaving responsibly and in socially appropriate ways in the classroom are causally related (Wentzel, 1991). In addition, the more challenging academic settings where students with greater social maturity tend to be placed have qualities, such as high expectations, that may contribute further to social maturity.

The tendency of students who are more socially competent to do better academically suggests that efforts to enhance the social development of the students can yield academic benefits (Wentzel, 1991). These efforts can include work with families to ensure that students have the requisite social skills by the time they enter educational programs (Greenberg, 1983) and the provision of social skills curriculum and intervention programs (Greenberg, Kusche, Calderon & Gustafson, 1983; Schloss & Smith, 1990) as part of the student's educational experiences.

What can be misleading in a consideration of this chapter is to think of deaf students' social experiences or orientations monolithicly. As Glickman (1986) and Gaustad and Kluwin (1992) have pointed out, deaf adolescents can represent quite different degrees of orientation to either peer group. In planning experiences that meet the needs of student populations with diverse social orientations, it is necessary for educators to keep in mind the independence of the two social orientations from each other. If a student has a strong interest in Deaf culture and a commitment to the deaf community, he or she *may* or *may not* want to also have hearing friends.

Our work on preferred associates in Chapter 5 is relevant to this point. The most frequently reported friendship pattern was to have a relatively good number of both hearing and deaf friends. Students with this pattern tended to have contact with many deaf peers, to be in programs where there was extensive mainstreaming, and to be good at both speaking and signing. We suggest that such students tended to have positive social orientations to *both* hearing and deaf peers. In addition to this group of students, as well as those strongly oriented to only one social group (either deaf or hearing), there are those who do not have a positive social orientation to either group. Approximately 14% of the students reported a friendship pattern with few friends, either deaf or hearing. Such students tended to be in programs with little mainstreaming, thus probably spending a large portion of their time in special classes, while also being poor signers. These students probably need special attention regarding social development (Asher *et al.,* 1990; Johnson, 1980).

Because social orientation is complex and level of interest in each social group varies from student to student, it is desirable for staff to support social activities and opportunities accordingly. For example, while there is a general favoritism of relationships with deaf schoolmates (Foster, 1989; Mertens, 1989; Stinson & Whitmire, 1991), our results indicate that some students found friendships with hearing peers rewarding and thus benefit from programming that includes opportunities for such relationships; however, in those cases considerable programmatic effort needs to be expended to create the structured opportunities on which friendships can be built between deaf and hearing peers. Within the deaf peers, the schools have a responsibility to expose the students to a broad range of experiences with Deaf culture.

Chapter 8

ACHIEVEMENT AND GRADE POINT AVERAGE

The achievement of deaf students in local public schools is influenced by student traits, instructional quality, and environmental influences (Walberg, 1984). Student traits would include ability or prior achievement, generally what is measured on standardized tests, and invariant traits such as hearing loss. Instructional quality involves two parameters: amount of instruction and quality of instruction. Environmental influences would include home and family influences and peer group relations.

Figure 8.1
A Modification of Walberg's (1984) Model of Schooling Effects

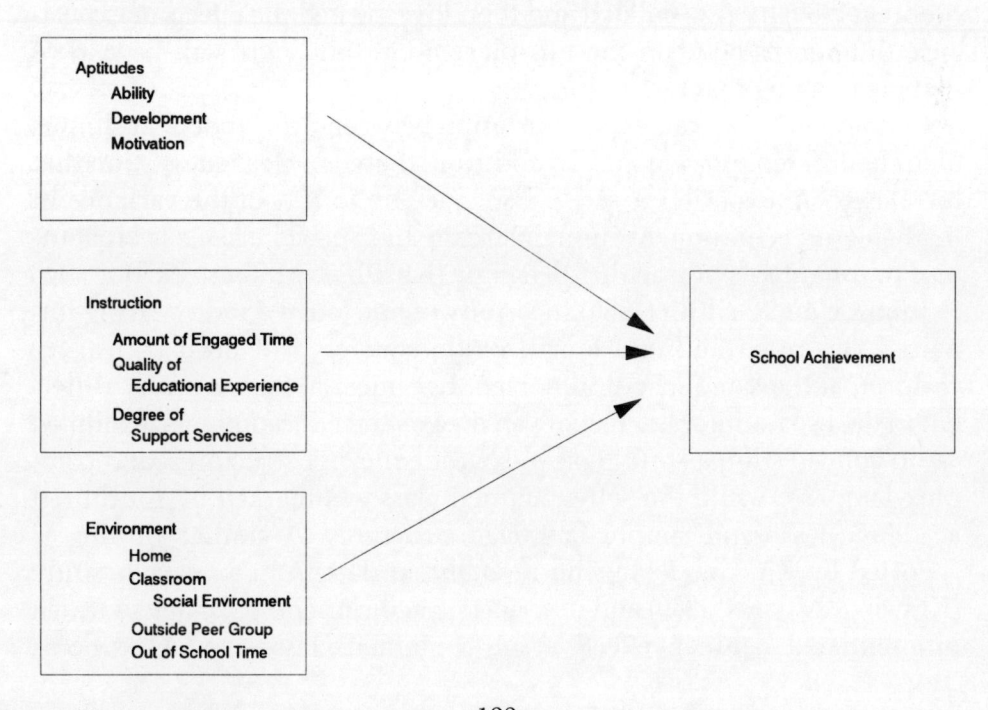

Aptitudes
  Ability
  Development
  Motivation

Instruction
  Amount of Engaged Time
  Quality of
    Educational Experience
  Degree of
    Support Services

Environment
  Home
  Classroom
    Social Environment
  Outside Peer Group
  Out of School Time

School Achievement

Considering student traits first, there are profound population differences, resulting from placement decisions, between the populations of the mainstream classes and the special classes for the deaf, including degree of hearing loss, ethnic background, age, and ability (Wolk et al., 1982). Less severely impaired students are more likely to be mainstreamed; black students are less likely to be mainstreamed; and as a child gets older, he or she is more likely to be mainstreamed (Wolk et al., 1982). Cumulatively, the demographic differences between these students are educationally significant and do count for a major portion of the variance in achievement between the two settings (Allen & Osborn, 1984; Kluwin & Moores, 1985; Kluwin and Moores, 1989).

A review of the work of Allen and Osborn (1984) and Kluwin and Moores (1985, 1989) suggests a fairly regular pattern in achievement studies of mainstreamed versus self-contained students. About 1% of the variance in achievement in short-term studies of achievement differences between mainstreamed and self-contained deaf students is attributable to the mainstream placement. However, between 20% and 25% of the variance in these studies can be attributed to initial demographic differences between the populations such as academic achievement, degree of hearing loss, additional handicapping conditions, and ethnicity. Of the remaining variance, the bulk is yet unexplained; however, Kluwin and Moores (1985) first speculated and then investigated the effects of experience differences between the two placements, but more will be said of that later in this chapter.

Consequently, we can expect variation between deaf students' achievement in different placements. In addition, there is a clear suggestion that the classroom experience varies also since up to 30% of the variance in mathematics achievement in mainstream and special classes is attributable to differences in teaching behavior (Kluwin & Moores, 1989).

Johnson and Griffith (1986) in a study of one fourth grade hearing impaired classroom and one fourth grade classroom of normal hearing children at the same school, reported that interactions were very different in the two settings. Interactions in the general education class exhibited rapid conversational shifts, complex academic task structures, and complex language while the self-contained class was marked by routinized academic tasks and simple language structures. A similar finding is reported by Kluwin (1992) who re-analyzed data from an earlier study (Kluwin & Moores, 1989) and described specific teaching behaviors which differentiated between effective self-contained classes and classrooms that were effective for mainstream students. Kluwin reported that there were general classroom process differences between mainstreamed mathematics classes and special classes. There was a tendency in the special classes toward individual forms of instruction as seen in a greater amount of seatwork and a higher degree of individualization. The successful mainstream class emphasized regular oral presentation by students and teachers and less seatwork. Larrivee (1985) has also noted similar differences between teachers who are effective with special students in mainstreamed classes and teachers who are not.

Unfortunately, the role of the interpreter in mainstream classes and its effects on student achievement remains largely unknown, but it can include not only interpreting but helping students with academic or social problems as well as being an instructional aide (Stedt, 1992). Unfortunately, few interpreters have adequate training for the diverse roles that are thrust upon them (Moores, Kluwin & Mertens, 1985; Rittenhouse, Rahn & Morreau, 1989). A "typical" interpreter would be a high school graduate with some college work and a brief training period and no certification or other assurance of skill (Mertens, 1985; Rittenhouse, Rahn & Morreau, 1989; Moores, Kluwin, & Mertens, 1985). While the role of the interpreter is critical, little information about the problem is available.

In an earlier chapter in this book, we discussed the importance of family influences on children's success in school, so there is little need to repeat that here. However, as we saw earlier, there is relatively little comparative family background data between students in segregated and mainstream placements although family influences are critical to later school achievement (Bodner-Johnson, 1985; Kluwin, & Gaustad, 1991, 1992).

Another environmental influence on children's achievement in school is the classroom social environment. The participation of deaf students with hearing and deaf classmates is a function of hearing status and degree of mainstreaming, but these factors operate independently of each other. For low to moderate levels of mainstreaming, participation with deaf peers increases. For high levels of mainstreaming, participation with deaf peers is severely reduced. Participation with hearing peers is unaffected by the degree of mainstreaming (Stinson & Whitmire, 1992). Identification with deaf peers grows as the degree of mainstreaming increases while identification with hearing peers is relatively level except for those deaf students who are mainstreamed for a great deal of time.

Stinson and Whitmire's (1992) findings are supported by Gaustad and Kluwin (1992) who reported that deaf students who are fully or nearly fully mainstreamed will develop an orientation towards hearing peers. For those who are not fully mainstreamed, the primary association remains with the deaf peer group. Although out-of-school contacts with deaf peers sometimes occur, the deaf peer group is mostly a school time phenomenon; consequently, it would appear that for the completely self-contained students the only peer group would be the deaf students in the class, thus making this a very powerful influence on their learning. For the fully mainstreamed deaf students, there would appear to be an affinity for the hearing peer group; however, we cannot suggest the impact of this peer group on the learning of the deaf students without information on their actual involvement with and acceptance by the hearing peers within a school.

Peer groups outside of school are likely to have little impact on deaf students since they spend relatively little time in their neighborhoods or interacting outside the classroom with peers. For example in Libbey and Pronovost's (1980) survey of hearing impaired adolescents mainstreamed in public schools, most of the deaf students reported that they did not frequently start conversations with hearing people, ask questions in class, or voluntarily answer questions. More than one quarter of the students listed making friends and communicating with hearing people as their biggest problem in school on an open-ended question, but most felt that hearing people did want to communicate with deaf people. Repeated studies (Raimondo & Maxwell, 1989; Saur *et al.,* 1980) have shown that even for highly mainstreamed and highly oral deaf students there is little social contact. We would expect little and highly variable influences of the outside peer group on the deaf child in the public school as well as quite different definitions of who are members of the peer group based on placement and communication mode use.

Applying Walberg's (1984) model of school achievement to deaf students in local public high schools, we could organize his categories of influences into three groups: those which have been shown to influence the achievement of deaf students, those which are as yet not shown to be related to school achievement, and those which do not contribute substantially. In our previous discussion, we focussed on the impact of these influences primarily in relation to the type of placement the child has experienced since this is the question that attracts the greatest degree of interest from the field.

Figure 8.2
A Model for Predicting Achievement

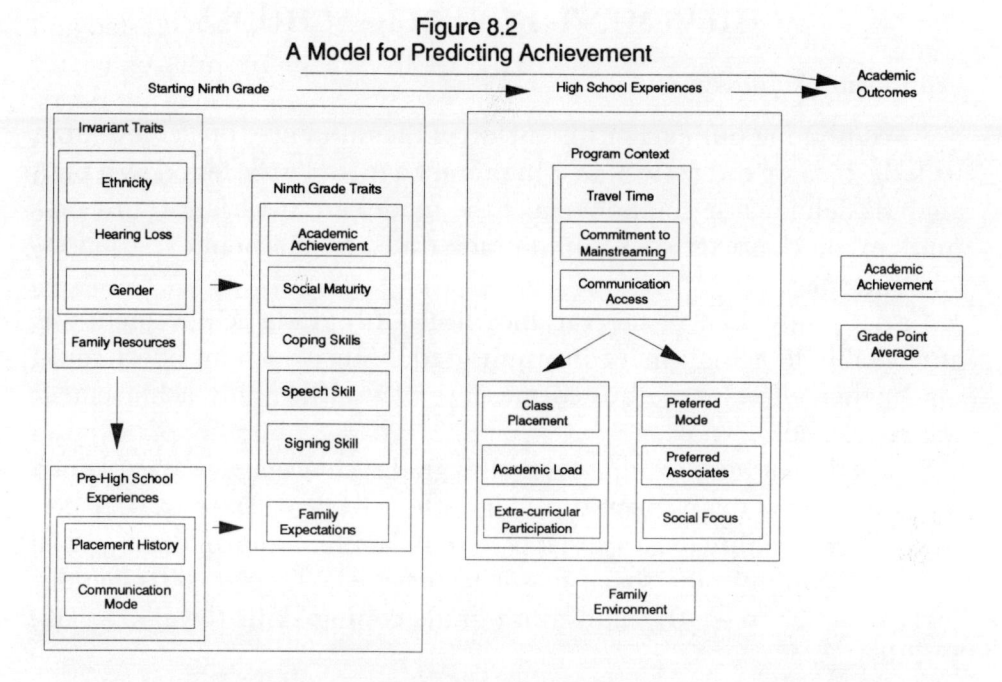

There is only one class of factors that consistently has been shown to influence achievement differences: pre-existing demographic or ability differences. Among the demographic differences, previous ability and race stand out as dominant influences on a child's later achievement. As to influences that are interesting but as yet have unsubstantiated effects on achievement, we would have to include family background, classroom teaching differences, and peer group influences. Recent work by Keith and Keith (1992) suggests that family influences while very interesting in the early grades are substantially mitigated by adolescence and as reported by Kluwin (in press) between class differences may be mitigated over time through the overall process of course selection. There are several components of Walberg's model that deserve more attention in the education of the deaf particularly the role of the interpreter. Peer group influences were discussed in Chapter 7.

In our study, we were able to collect information on some but not all of the influences in Walberg's model. In those areas where we were able to collect information, we found results similar to what was reported in earlier studies.

ACHIEVEMENT IN PUBLIC SCHOOLS

Composite Achievement

By combining our earlier discussion of the influences on achievement with the data we did collect, we can present a model to be tested by a path analysis. The major components of the model are invariant traits, pre-ninth grade characteristics, ninth grade traits, high school experiences, and outcomes.

In our study, 27% of the variance in twelfth grade achievement was attributable to achievement in ninth grade. Since such an effect could mask other effects, an adjusted measure of twelfth grade achievement was computed.

39% of the variance in adjusted twelfth grade achievement was explained by the amount of mainstreaming in high school (beta = .252; $p < .001$), perceived speech ability (beta = .311; $p < .001$), family resources (beta = .248; $p < .001$), ninth grade social maturity (beta = .198; $p < .001$), gender (beta = −.125; $p < .01$), and ninth grade coping skills (beta = −.112; $p < .01$).

The relationship between high school placement and adjusted achieve-

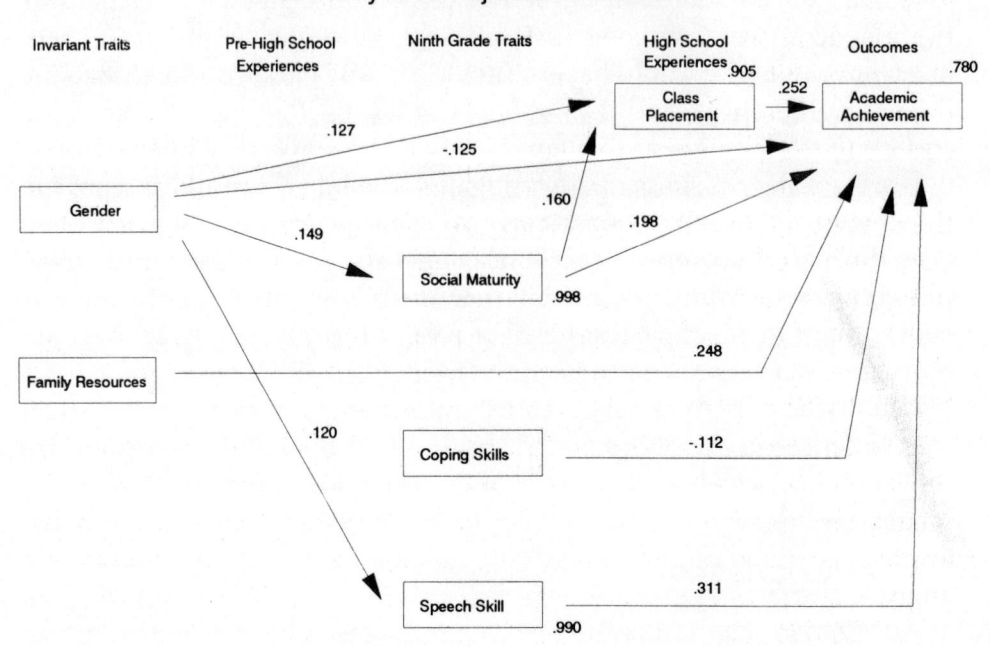

Figure 8.3
Path Analysis for Adjusted Achievement

ment divided the sample into four groups from lowest to highest adjusted achievement: full time in special classes, single class mainstream placement, some multiple class mainstream placement, and regular placement in several mainstream classes. We mentioned at the beginning of this chapter the relationship between academic achievement and class placement. Numerous studies have noted that the primary if not sole determinant used by school programs for mainstream placement of deaf students is the student's academic ability. In our model academic ability enters into the prediction of achievement and later in the analysis of cumulative grade point average in two ways. First, higher achieving students are more likely to be placed in mainstream classes. Second, academic achievement will facilitate further academic achievement. School achievers are school achievers because they are brighter and more motivated. The cumulative effect of achievement is more achievement.

Visual inspection of the plots of the relationship between speech skill and achievement, between family resources and achievement, and between ninth grade social maturity and achievement suggests that the relationship in all cases is generally linear with the difference in effect size being due to more dispersion of the scores rather than any apparent nonlinearity in the data. In other words, for many, but not all deaf students, higher levels of family resources, better perceived speech skill, and greater ninth grade maturity will mean higher levels of achievement in twelfth grade.

Social maturity operates in an interesting way in this model but in an even more complex way in predicting cumulative grade point average, so we will discuss it in more detail below.

The higher achieving modal graduate of a public school program for the deaf would be a male who, of course, started high school as a higher achieving student, had been in more mainstream classes, had good perceived speech skills, had a better educated mother or more affluent family than the norm, and started high school more socially mature.

Grade Point Average

Like achievement, grade point average could be heavily influenced by the student's initial achievement level. Although, ninth grade achievement only accounted for 5% of the variance in cumulative grade point average, adjusted rather than actual grade point average was used in our analysis.

Adjusted grade point average was accounted for by high school place-

Figure 8.4
Path Analysis for Adjusted Grade Point Average

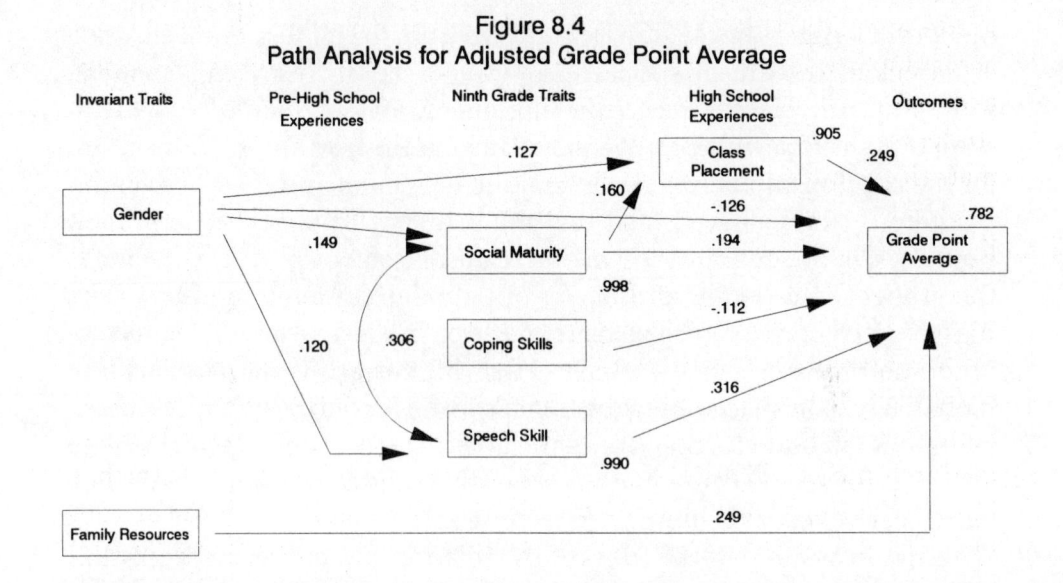

ment (beta = .249; p < .001), ninth grade speech ability (beta = .316; p < .001), family resources (beta = .249; p < .001), ninth grade social maturity (beta = .193; p < .001), and gender (beta = −.126; p < .005). This accounted for about 40% of the variance in adjusted grade point average.

The relationship between high school placement and adjusted grade point average divided the sample into four groups from lowest to highest adjusted grade point average: full time in special classes, single class mainstream placement, some multiple class mainstream placement, and regular placement in several mainstream classes.

Visual inspection of the plots of the relationship between speech skill and adjusted grade point average and between family resources and adjusted grade point average suggests that the relationship in both cases is generally linear with the difference in effect size being due to dispersion of the scores, that is, a generally weak relationship rather than one with a particular "break" point. Adjusted grade point average is influenced by perceived speech skill and family resources in the same way as achievement is influenced, that is, it applies for many but not all students.

Ninth grade social maturity contributed less to this relationship because the relationship is not quite linear. For students with an adjusted grade point average above 2.6, the relationship is generally linear and positive. For students with an adjusted grade point average below 2.6, there appears to be no particular relationship between social maturity in ninth grade and adjusted grade point average. In other words, for higher achieving students there is a relationship between their grade point average, their ability, and their social maturity. For lower achieving students, grade point average is somewhat related to ability but social maturity is unrelated to grade point average.

Social maturity influences cumulative grade point average and to a lesser degree cumulative achievement in other ways than directly. Social maturity in ninth grade is a key factor in the decision to mainstream a student. Since mainstreaming through its emphasis on greater academic work influences achievement, social maturity in ninth grade has a secondary effect on cumulative grade point average and achievement. More mature students also tend to take more courses. While increased course load reduces grade point average, social maturity in ninth grade further influences cumulative grade point average. Put simply, the more mature student—as perceived by the teachers—is one who is adjusted to the school culture. This individual functions well in the school setting which can be seen in both greater school responsibility and higher levels of success as measured by school standards.

Males had higher adjusted grade point averages; however, gender has another influence on grade point average by influencing ninth grade social maturity. Females are generally perceived as more mature in the ninth grade, and individuals who are more mature in the ninth grade tend to have higher grade point averages. In other words, there are gender effects in this system, but the relationships are not simple. It would seem that females have some advantage before high school while males have an advantage during high school.

The typical student with a high cumulative grade point average would be a young man who had been extensively mainstreamed, had good speech skills, a better educated mother, and was more socially mature in the ninth grade. This is similar to the typical student with high twelfth grade achievement.

The Inter-Relationship of Some Ninth Grade Traits

There is a sequence of relationships among several of the ninth grade traits across all of the analyses that should be discussed together because they present us with the appearance of types of students. Measures of academic achievement are related to perceived speech skill and social maturity. Social maturity is in turn related to coping skills. Achievement, social maturity, and perceived speech skills share on the average about

15% of their mutual variance with coping skills sharing about 3% of its variance with social maturity. This means that there are groups of students who would be socially mature, high achieving, and who would have good speech. In real life, they would stand out in any program and be readily identified. At the same time, there are students who are lower achieving, immature, and who have poor speech skills. Again, if one mentioned this set of traits to a teacher of the deaf, he or she could probably cite examples from his or her own experience.

The point to be made is that while these factors overlap completely in some cases and are obvious when they do, it does not mean that they are totally linked. For example, it would be possible to locate in our data set, high achieving students with good speech skills who were very immature or high achieving and quite mature students who had unintelligible speech. The set of variables are related and do influence later achievement, but they are not a guarantee of success if high nor a curse if low because they are only partially related. In other words, in the ninth grade, a mature student with strong academic skills and good speech is more likely to succeed than an immature student with weak academic skills and unintelligible speech; however, the former student may do no better than another skilled and mature student who does not have intelligible speech. At the end of this book, we will reiterate this point, that is, there is sufficient shared variance among some variables to evoke memories of individuals, but the association of the variables is tenuous enough to allow for many exceptions.

Components of Overall Achievement

Progress in Reading Comprehension.

Ninth grade reading comprehension predicts 35% of the variance in twelfth grade reading comprehension. When this variance is removed, 50% of the variance in adjusted twelfth grade reading comprehension can be predicted using race, family resources, ninth grade social maturity, coping skills, speech skills, signing skills, family environment during high school, and degree of mainstreaming during high school. This collection of variables suggests several language related variables account for the change in reading comprehension.

Reading comprehension as measured in this study was the ability to comprehend written English; consequently, measures of English skills would be expected to be strongly related to twelfth grade reading comprehension. It is no surprise that the largest predictor of twelfth grade reading comprehension is ninth grade reading comprehension. The learning curve for reading, probably identical to writing at the beginning, is much sharper in the early grades than it is for mathematics while in the later grades mathematics can show a steady or even rapid expansion in knowledge as one progresses from the rudimentary to the advanced. At the same time, sophistication in composition can become more elaborate because of the expanded knowledge base offered by one's reading ability. This translates into ninth grade reading comprehension having more predictive power than other measures of ninth grade academic ability.

The perspective to take on the substantial contribution of perceived ninth grade speech skill is to ask whether or not this reflects the quality of the individual's speech or the individual's knowledge of English since both constructs would be involved in self-reports of oral language skills. Since ninth grade reading skill correlates with speech skill and degree of hearing loss does not enter into the model, we could reasonably assert that in this case perceived speech skill was better understood as a surrogate for English language skill.

Signing skill is negatively related to class placement and to reading comprehension. In this environment, students who use more sign language tend to be those who are in more restricted settings. The relationship between signing skill and placement and reading comprehension, no doubt, reflects the generally weaker English proficiency of these students.

Degree of mainstreaming divides change in reading comprehension into three groups. Students who were mainstreamed regularly had the highest adjusted reading scores (scaled score mean = 651.5), students who were occasionally mainstreamed had the second highest (scaled score mean = 629.4), and all of the other students formed a single cluster (scaled score mean = 612.8).

Race divided adjusted reading scores into two groups: whites and non-whites. The average adjusted scaled score for white students was 633.5 while it was 610 for non-white students. This reinforces the general impression that twelfth grade reading achievement is related to ninth grade language levels since white students were higher on ninth grade reading achievement and perceived speech skill than minority students. Family resources and ethnicity are mildly related. Part of the effect of ethnicity must be attributed to family education levels and probably to a family's access to services or products that would assist the deaf child with access to more information about the world. Both of these factors would be strongly related to the financial resources of the family.

Changes in Writing Quality.

Between ninth grade and twelfth grade students improved across the board in their writing skills.

Table 8.1
SOME MEASURES OF WRITING QUALITY

	Grade 9	Grade 12
Words per clause	5.47	6.10
Clauses per t-unit	1.72	1.67
% Correct clauses	36.3%	47.4%

The syntactic complexity of the students' writing did improve with time as can be seen in the words per clause index; however, it would appear that a reversal occurred in the clauses per t-unit measure. It needs to be pointed out that the clauses per t-unit measure includes both grammatical and ungrammatical clauses. While the number of clauses per t-unit apparently declined, the number of correct clauses increased. What in effect occurred is that students' written English syntax became slightly more complex at the phrase level, remained about the same at the sentence level but became more grammatically correct. An entry/exit consideration of the measures of rhetorical quality also showed across the board improvements in the persuasive letter, the descriptive essay, and the business letter.

Mathematics Achievement.

Mathematics Computation. Ninth grade mathematics computation predicted 23% of the variance in twelfth grade mathematics computation. 23% of the variance of adjusted twelfth grade mathematics computation was predicted by gender, family resources, ninth grade social maturity, and degree of mainstreaming in high school. If the results of this analysis could be summarized, aside from the degree of mainstreaming, family resources and gender impact mathematics computation skills. Males (adjusted scaled score = 684.9) achieved slightly better than females (adjusted scaled score = 682.2).

Mathematics computation produces a sparse picture when compared to mathematics concept achievement or reading comprehension. Unfortunately, this path analysis is the least descriptive of all of the analyses in the sense the smallest amount of variance is accounted for. One possibility is that there is some kind of "ceiling effect" for this skill, particularly for the higher achieving students.

Mathematics Concepts

27% of the variance in twelfth grade mathematics concepts is accounted for by ninth grade mathematics concepts. 36% of adjusted twelfth grade achievement is predicted by coping skills in ninth grade, ninth grade speech skills, gender, family expectation, family affluence, and ninth grade social maturity. The structure of the variables which predict change in mathematics concepts seem more like the variables in the prediction of reading skills than for mathematics computation.

Conclusion

If you were an oralist, you can find justification for the teaching of speech in elementary schools by citing the relationship between perceived speech skill in ninth grade and twelfth grade achievement. If you were an honest oralist, you would have to also accept the burden of explaining the inter-relationship of ethnicity, gender, speech skill, and achievement. Since the authors of this book both have intelligible speech, but are not oralists, we do not feel any particular commitment to that version of the "truth." Our truth consists of clusters and wiggles rather than straight lines because ultimately this is a correlational study which can only suggest the truth, not substantiate it.

Some clusters are family resources and ethnicity, or achievement and degree of hearing loss. An example of a wiggle would be the relationship between social maturity and school achievement.

The problem with clusters is that some of these clusters such as family resources and ethnicity arrive in schools and we cannot change them. Some clusters arrive in schools and we should encourage them such as the relationship between early exposure to information, either spoken, signed, or printed, and achievement. Sometimes, through good programming, we can overcome the limits of one cluster by supplying another. For example, head start programs for deaf minority students would help to overcome some of the early effects of ethnicity on achievement.

Wiggles are a problem for policy planners or anyone else trying to organize a program. Wiggles are relationships that are not strictly linear. For example, social maturity only provides an added "boost" to the achievement of deaf students when they are operating above a C average. For students below a C average, a program in junior high aimed at making them more socially ready for high school is probably a waste of effort.

This chapter has provided considerable information on what influences the achievement of deaf students in local public schools. Returning to our model at the beginning, we would see that again demographic influences are important. Of course, some issues such as interpreting are still left unanswered. In the process of using Walberg's (1984) model in looking at the achievement of deaf high school students, we have seen that we are left with some thorny problems.

What this chapter could not do, because of wiggles and clusters, is give a simple account of what occurred. For example, one way to look at the local public high school is as a hearing person's environment. Thus, one way to envision the successful deaf student is to see that individual as being "more like a hearing person" to begin with. Such a view would place an emphasis on the contribution of speech skill to the overall picture of achievement. This view would be reinforced if degree of hearing loss and sign language use were also included in the prediction model, but they do not show up. Therefore, we need another way to look at the deaf child who is an academic success in the local high school. We could look at this individual as a successful ninth grader. This successful ninth grader could read at or near grade level, was socially mature, and had a highly supportive family who expected the child to succeed. The advantage of the successful student view, as opposed to the hearing person view, is that it subsumes more of the components of the various prediction models that we have seen in this chapter. In a discussion of success in school as measured by school standards, being skilled, working hard, cooperating with the system, and having helpful parents go a long way to explaining why some achieve and others don't.

Chapter 9

GAINING A PERSPECTIVE ON THE PUBLIC SCHOOL EXPERIENCE

In this chapter we will attempt to do three things. First, we will try to create a feeling for the experience that these students had by going beyond the data and sharing some of our more memorable experiences. Second, we will return to the data but at a higher level than we discussed in the previous chapters in order to identify some dominant themes. Finally, we will offer our thoughts on the meaning of what we have found.

SNAPSHOTS FROM THE LONGITUDINAL STUDY

At the beginning of this book, we described some typical children to make the complexity of the education of deaf children in local public schools more real. Here again, we need to pause and re-insert into the discussion the face of individuals and the texture of events.

Subways and Deafness

This project was based on the notion of reciprocal interaction between a research team and school administrators as a way to collect data and develop useful innovations (Kluwin, 1991). One result of this philosophy were periodic meetings at the school sites on a rotating basis. During one of these meetings, the research team and the administrators of some of the programs were introduced to some "typical" deaf students from the program. After a very strained hour with the students doing their best to use their speech, the students were allowed to go home. Blessedly, the research team and the school administrators called it quits shortly thereafter.

The adults, both deaf and hearing, arrived on the local subway platform to find a much more relaxed group of adolescents with their voices shut off and their fingers flying. As we all got onto the same train, the students began to sort out some clearer ideas about our group, particularly that there were deaf adults in charge of programs for the deaf and working in hearing universities and that some hearing people really could sign. What they give us back was an insight into the lives of urban, deaf adolescents.

Urban deaf adolescents are like adolescents every place else. They love to hang out with each other. In Washington, D.C. or Toronto, Canada or Philadelphia where there are good subway systems, the kids jump on the subway on the weekend and head for a particular stop: Union Station in DC or the Bloor Street Metro stop in Toronto. In San Antonio, we found them on the Riverwalk at a particular bridge over the river. Our team was always as surprised as the kids to find each other. Fingers would flash; names were exchanged; and questions flew.

When we talked about creating opportunities for interaction and the need for a deaf community for the deaf child in the local public school, we were thinking about these kids. Given a solution to the problem of a low incidence handicap—safe, rapid public transit—and the human need for peer association, these children could construct their own system. However, that particular solution was not common to every program site we visited.

The Girl in the Green Garbage Bag

Homecoming week is not a good time to do data collection in schools. However, when you are trying to patch together a longitudinal study on a limited or sometimes non-existent budget you go places when someone else is willing to pay your way. That is how we met the girl in the green garbage bag.

On this particular field test of one of our data collection instruments, we had to first discuss the quality of the decorations on the classroom door before we could begin since the day before had been door decoration day as part of "Spirit Week." Today, was "Punk" day. Kids were roaming around the building wearing multicolored hair, shredded clothing, and safety pins in strange places. Black was a dominant color and leather the preferred fabric.

Out of the entire melange of images, one persists. There was a pretty deaf girl with short chestnut hair wearing a black body stocking, a black beret, and a green trash bag strategically cut, tucked, and fluffed. I asked this apparition why she was wearing a garbage bag. Her reply was, "Punks like trashy things. What is trashier than a garbage bag."

Band Wallies

Adolescents are tribal. In one high school that housed an oral program for the deaf, some conversations with students turned up nearly a dozen "tribes." "Band Wallies" were people who took two periods of music each day, came to school early for marching band practice, and stayed late for orchestra practice. Another group were the "Skate rats" and the "Skate betty poseurs". Skateboarding is a male phenomenon, possibly one of the last bastions of chauvinism outside of English men's clubs, certain religious orders in Greece, and professional football. Skate betty poseurs were the girls who hung around the skate rats, usually playing with their hair. "Druggies" were known for their glassy looks, scraggly hair, and flannel shirts as opposed to "metal heads" who had scraggly hair and black t-shirts. "New wave" rose and receded during the course of our study but seemed to center around people wearing black clothing made out of natural fabrics and listening to music that sounded like it had been taped in someone's garage. "Bops" were the well-dressed and carefully coiffed young people who dominated school politics, the honor roll, and homecoming or prom. Of course, there were also "jocks" and "rednecks" or "townies" depending on the location. Ethnic or racial minorities also banded together unless there were large numbers of them, then they split into groups usually on the basis of family affluence or length of time in the country. Deaf students who "fit in" did so as members of one of the "tribes." Acceptance of peer standards and outstanding personal characteristics brought integration.

Lunch Time

The school cafeteria is one of the horrors of public education that both binds and divides the students. It binds them in a camaraderie of misery, but it also shows the divisions among them in some very unpleasant ways.

Periodically, members of the research team were forced either by time or transportation constraints to eat in the school cafeteria. While suffering this fate, we often watched our surroundings. One school summed up many of the barriers that need to be overcome.

It was a moderately sized school cafeteria added to the building almost as an after thought so it stuck out from the building which gave it windows on two sides. You entered it from the school building and immediately faced the serving area. Over the entrance to most school cafeterias, there should be the quotation from Dante, "Abandon hope, all ye who enter here." The food was average, that is, barely edible and certainly not digestible.

As you entered, you were confronted by a wide central aisle which divided the rows of tables in half. On the left hand side near the doors sat virtually every black student in the school. On the right hand side near the serving area, the sounds of Spanish drifted back towards the door. Fingers flew up in the left hand corner of the cafeteria while a small group of white students spoke quietly among themselves in the opposite corner.

Mainstream Math Class

A mainstream math class starts with a warm-up problem while the teacher takes attendance and sorts out administrative problems in the class. The problem and the quiet time is over in five to ten minutes. Next the teacher reviews the homework. This is done by picking on individual students to give the answers to specific problems. If you're smart, you've done your homework already and you correct your answers as needed. In most classes, trying and being wrong is infinitely preferable to not trying. The next item on the agenda is new material. Most math curricula proceed in small steps that are reviewed regularly. This "lecture" seldom lasts longer than ten minutes. The last major block of time is devoted to the assignment of homework, the explanation and demonstration of a few problems, and time for students to get started. Some students will finish their homework in class; however, the teacher uses this time to go around the room and answer questions as well as check on how students are progressing.

During this class the interpreter has varying degrees of success. While the deaf students are doing the challenge problem, the interpreter has some "down time". Most interpreters deserve this because once the round robin of correcting homework starts, it is a real challenge to keep up with the rapid pace of identifying who is talking, interpreting the question, and giving the answer. This is also a demanding time for the deaf student who must look up and down from his or her paper to check his or her homework and catch the next answer. The pace is furious and demanding. It is also the pace at which a large volume of research has shown that students learn more math (Kluwin and Moores, 1989).

The lecture portion of the class is a more "normal" interpreting situation in that the straight monologue of the teacher gives a simpler focus point for the student and the interpreter. Of course, the pace of the lecture and the familiarity of the content will influence the quality of the interpreting. While the students start on their homework, different interpreter roles will be seen in different classes. In some cases the interpreter will tutor the deaf student while in others both will wait for the teacher to come around.

Deaf Students' Complaints

At ninth grade and at twelfth grade, personal concerns account for about a quarter of all complaints. After four years of school experience, the lunchroom has become the focus of many of the students' complaints. One student in six during ninth grade was troubled by the cafeteria situation. By twelfth grade, nearly one student in four was concerned about it. Half again as many students were concerned with personal safety in twelfth grade as were in ninth grade. The focus of the ninth grade comments were to a large extent about being bullied or confrontations with hearing students. By twelfth grade, the concern was over guns and drugs. Consistently, one student in eight was concerned about improving the physical environment of the school. These concerns ranged from painting over ugly walls to the stench in the restrooms. Deafness related topics concerned one child in fourteen, but restrictive school policies were the nemesis of many children. In the ninth grade, the complaints were frequently related to having to get up earlier to go to school while by twelfth grade the complaints had changed to a lack of freedom, particularly not being allowed to go out at lunch time. Complaints about teachers grew from barely 2% in ninth grade to 6% in the twelfth grade. Again, the theme of the veteran versus the neophyte emerges.

Ninth grade was typified by a concern with personal problems, other kids picking on them, the adjustment to a new school with regrets about leaving behind the old school as well as some optimism about how good things could be if "only...." Twelfth grade reflected the concern of the veteran of the high school experience. There was less optimism about making constructive changes and the concerns for personal safety have moved from big-kids-bother-me to drugs and guns in the schools.

In the twelfth grade, deafness related topics were more or less evenly divided among all of the programs. Strictness of rules was a concern of black deaf students in one program and white students in two affluent suburban programs. Personal safety was a concern of white students from blue collar families in an integrated program; various students in one large urban program; and all students in two locations in the Southwest. Issues of personal comfort were raised by the students in the poorest and in the most affluent programs. Cafeterias and school food were universally reviled.

School programs based on the students' comments had particular flavors. One program was seen as stifling; another was a dangerous place to be because of the random violence in the school; another was a collection of petty nuisances suffered by harassed adolescents with less than good grace; one program that one of the authors can attest to from personal experience had the worst food of any school in North America with half of the students in twelfth grade making a point of mentioning it in their essays.

As these "snapshots" show, while we "turned students into numbers" for percentages, regressions, and path analyses, that is not how we really remember them. We remember the students as real kids, and we remember them vividly—their fears, their gripes, and their costumes. Experiences with the students, teachers, and programs "hit us harder" and were "more meaningful" than any numerical results. Being in a lunch room where most of the students are black, hispanic, or deaf makes a much stronger impression on you than any data on percentages of students from various ethnic groups.

LOOKING AT THE RESULTS

We interpret the results in the context of the strong impressions gained from the visits to the schools and their students. The results bore out many important influences on the development of the students in the school setting that would never have been noticed had we relied on observation and experience alone. The results made clear that no simple explanation of the academic and social development of the students is possible. The major indicators of development were multiply determined; and each of these multiple determinants did not exert a simple, linear effect on development but, rather, interacted with other factors. Adding to this complexity, there were chains of influence. For example (and as elaborated upon below) elementary school placement appeared to depend on family characteristics and the nature of the student's hearing impairment. Subsequent high school placement seemed to depend on elementary placement. In turn, high school achievement, and to some extent social development, were dependent on high school placement.

The first cluster of variables we should consider are the invariant traits of ethnicity, degree of hearing loss, gender, and family resources.

Ethnicity is a frequent but relatively low intensity variable in predicting the various components of the model in that it explains from 1% to 6% of the variance in the prediction equations in which it appears. It has its greatest impact earlier in the child's education since it contributes to elementary school placement decisions, elementary school communication mode use, ninth grade perceived speaking skill, and ninth grade achievement. Black and hispanic children are more likely to be in special classes during elementary school, be in total communication programs during elementary school, have lower ninth grade achievement levels, and lower perceived speech skills than their white or asian peers. During high school, black and hispanic students are more likely to remain in special classes, take more academic courses, and more likely to be oriented toward hearing peers than their white or asian peers. However, about 25% of the variance in ethnicity is attributable to family resources and vice versa.

Family resources impacts elementary school variables in the same way ethnicity does but impacts high school variables like gender does. Family resources, that is family income and parental education, positively impacts elementary school placement and communication mode use, 2% to 4.4% of the variance. It predicts 3% of the variance in ninth grade achievement, but predicts 6% of twelfth grade achievement that has been adjusted for ninth grade achievement meaning that it impacts achievement both directly and cumulatively. It also accounts for 6% of the variance in adjusted cumulative grade point average. The family's education level and capacity to provide more financial resources to the deaf child is a pervasive predictor of school success.

Hearing loss is an infrequent predictor with a variable range of effects from 2% to about 18% of the variance. It impacts on elementary school educational choices, perceived speech skill and orientation towards deaf peers. A less severe hearing loss means that the child is more likely to be mainstreamed during elementary school, more likely to be in an oral program, have a higher perceived speaking ability, and less likely to be oriented to deaf peers.

Gender exhibits no effects in the analysis until high school, but then impacts several of the nine variables in the analysis. Females are more likely to have higher perceived speech skills, more likely to be mainstreamed, less likely to participate in extra-curriculars, more likely to have an orientation toward deaf peers, and are more mature in twelfth grade than males. Gender effects are quite noticeable in outcome measures. Males have higher twelfth grade achievement levels and cumulative grade point averages when those measures are adjusted for ninth grade achievement than females. Males are also more likely to be oriented toward hearing peers. Gender effects vary from less than 1% of the variance for orientation to deaf peers to nearly 4% of the variance for extra-curricular participation in high school, making it a persistent low level effect throughout high school.

Elementary school placement and communication mode use share 7.5% of their variance. They also impact many of the same high school variables: ninth grade maturity, perceived speech skill, and high school placement. Students who were more heavily mainstreamed in elementary school and who attended oral programs tended to have higher ninth grade maturity, higher perceived speech skill, and were more likely to be mainstreamed. However, since these elementary school placement decisions are also influenced by the ethnicity and degree of hearing loss of the children and these same effects persist in the prediction equations for ninth grade maturity, perceived speech skill, and high school placement, we cannot declare oral education or elementary school mainstreaming a resounding success. For some deaf children oral education and mainstream placements are having a positive impact, but that population has some specific characteristics not related to educational practice. With the exception of perceived signing skill, most of the variance explained by these two placement decisions ranges from 2% to 6%.

Many of the various measures of ninth grade skills are reciprocal with each other, accounting for between 6% and 22% of their mutual variance.

Ninth grade achievement determines placement type and degree of extra-curricular participation in high school. In addition it has a substantial impact on twelfth grade achievement and cumulative grade point average directly and indirectly. It also influences twelfth grade social maturity directly and through its relationship with ninth grade social maturity. It is a powerful but limited variable in this analysis.

Social maturity in ninth grade accounts for 2.5% of the variance in class placement during high school. In addition, it accounts for nearly 4% of the variance in adjusted twelfth grade achievement and adjusted cumulative grade point average. Because social maturity in ninth grade has a substantial effect on social maturity in twelfth grade, twelfth grade social maturity was adjusted for it.

Family expectations is reciprocal with ninth grade achievement and social maturity, but the only variable it predicts is high school placement. Parents with high expectations for their children have children who have higher levels of ninth grade achievement, are more mature in ninth grade, and are more likely to be placed in mainstream classes. As Keith and Keith (1992) have noted, family influences on school achievement diminish after elementary school.

Perceived speech skill is an academic achievement predictor while perceived signing skill is a social outcome predictor. Perceived speech skill predicts adjusted twelfth grade achievement and adjusted cumulative grade point average. Perceived signing skill predicts extra-curricular participation and orientation to peers. Higher perceived speech skills is related to higher adjusted twelfth grade achievement and adjusted cumulative grade point average. Higher perceived signing skill predicts more extra-curricular participation, a stronger orientation to deaf peers, and a weaker orientation to hearing peers.

Degree of mainstreaming impacts all of the outcome measures except orientation to deaf peers. It predicts around 4% to 6% of the variance in adjusted twelfth grade achievement, cumulative grade point average, social maturity, and orientation to hearing peers.

Another way of looking at the overall results of the longitudinal study is to consider the results from the perspective of individual students. In this way, one extreme tends to emerge: the less hearing impaired, more affluent white student in a suburban school district who has been extensively mainstreamed and has had considerable exposure to oral education. The other extreme is defined by a poor black or hispanic child. The black child is less likely to have a consistent communication philosophy but is more likely to be placed in a special class while the hispanic child is placed in a total communication program and tracked for special classes. By ninth grade both types of children have poor speech skills and lower achievement. Consequently, they tend to be kept in special classes throughout high school and finish with poorer social skills and lower achievement. This dichotomy is overly simplistic since it misses blue collar, white children and middle class black children as well as misses the variety of programming structures even within this study.

IDEAS WE CANNOT AVOID

Racism, Persistent and Pernicious

Race is a pernicious factor in the school achievement of deaf students. While it contributed a greater percentage to ninth grade achievement than to twelfth grade achievement, it was a substantial factor in predicting the achievement of these adolescents. In a separate analysis, it was found that about 25% of the variance in ethnicity is related to family resource differences such as mother's level of education, overall family income, and the possession of technology which mediates the communication problems of deafness such as telecommunications devices and caption decoders (Kluwin & Gaustad, 1992). In other words, white deaf adolescents tended to have mothers who were better educated, more affluent, and more likely to own deafness-related telecommunication devices. Black deaf adolescents and hispanic deaf adolescents had less well-educated mothers and were less affluent; however, hispanic deaf adolescents were at a greater disadvantage than black deaf adolescents.

We cannot dismiss the pervasiveness of racism in American society; however, we must be careful in selecting the point at which we fix blame. Deaf minority students come to schools less advantaged than white students. Public legislation and regulation as well as a general concern of the profession for equity in education mediates against overt racism in programming decisions. While subtle forms of racism may appear in programming decisions for deaf minority members, such information does not appear to be extractable from the data set.

Several sources for lower achievement among some deaf youngsters might be identified including generalized race or class or cultural values toward education, access to assistive services, and attitudes toward communication modes. White and asian students achieved better than black or hispanic students. Recently, there has been some documentation on the reasons for asian immigrant achievement (Caplan *et al.*, 1992) which include a family emphasis on doing well in school and specific supports for achievement, factors which Bodner-Johnson (1986) and Kluwin and Gaustad (1992) have shown to be important for deaf adolescents' achievement. A second factor is that lower family incomes result in reduced access to social and medical services which might mitigate some of the communication deficits of deafness. For example, less affluent families are less likely to spend scarce resources on a telecommunications device for a deaf child. Or less access to medical help or social services can result in a later identification of a hearing loss which results in delayed remediation and hence lower school achievement. Thirdly, as Kluwin and Gaustad (1991) have pointed out, educated white mothers are more likely to learn and use manual communication with a deaf child than less educated or minority group mothers. This lack of within family communication can also reduce school achievement by depriving the child of needed school achievement support from the family (Kluwin & Gaustad, 1992).

However, even the above discussion is potentially racist if it ignores blue collar white families who also have difficulties responding to the demands of a handicapped child or black families that surround and support a deaf child all the way to a graduate degree. Race, as a marker for a constellation of related variables, was a factor in the achievement of these adolescents, but the assignment of responsibility is not a simple matter.

The Role of the Family

Some of what produces differences in deaf graduates of local public schools is family affluence and parental education levels. Better educated parents with more economic resources are more able to respond to the child's hearing loss in a positive fashion. For families who are living from paycheck to paycheck or welfare check to welfare check, the demands of a special child no doubt overwhelm a fragile system. Unfortunately in American society and in our study, family affluence and parental education were confounded with race.

Some of the problem may lie in family stability. Among the 60% of the respondents to the parent questionnaire, about one-quarter were divorced or single parents. When we solicited marital status information from the schools for the remaining 40%, nearly 9 out of 10 parents were identified as divorced or single parents. A single parent raising a child is a monumental task, but a single parent raising several children including one who is deaf is a task beyond appreciation.

In a way, we, as members of the school establishment, can take some solace from all this by saying that these are factors that we have no control over and have to "live with it." But from the research team's experience in working with some very dedicated school personnel trying to cope with the problems of urban education during the nineteen-eighties, this is a very cold comfort.

Sexism

Sex differences were also a frequently noted variable in the longitudinal study, particularly the "rollover" effect of girls being higher than boys in ninth grade but falling behind the boys in twelfth grade. Currently, there is an active research tradition looking at these very same effects in general education. Explanations vary from general cultural values which work against women to cognitive processing differences between men and women to different gender responses during adolescence to puberty.

Our study generated enough information to note the differences in the areas of extra-curricular participation, achievement, social maturity, and peer orientation. Unfortunately, we did not collect appropriate data to explain these differences. Nonetheless, it is apparent that deaf girls start high school performing differently than boys, have different school experiences, and different outcomes at the end. This is one area of research that needs immediate attention.

THINGS THAT WORKED AND THINGS THAT DIDN'T WORK

In spite of the impediments they have faced, the determined teachers, administrators, and support staff in the 15 programs have made headway in developing the students' academic and social skills and in preparing them for life after high school. Even if a program was inadequately funded and attended by an inner city population, it could offer better academic and vocational preparation than anyone would have have reason to expect. Even if loneliness and isolation are very real problems in schools where students are mainstreamed, programs in the study found effective ways of supporting their students' social development.

Working Towards Work

Because of our close relationship with the school administrators, the biased nature of our sample at the program level, in the sense, that this is a volunteer sample, and the small total number of programs (15), we did not attempt to specifically evaluate any program. Nonetheless, in the process of compiling and analyzing all of the data in this study, it was not possible to miss differences among the programs.

One particular difference was true of the two "poorest" programs of the 15. You would have to define "poorest" in the sense of the programs whose kids had the lowest family incomes, the highest percentage of single parent families, the greatest percentage of non-English speaking parents, and the lowest program average ninth grade achievement scores. These kids would have been a challenge to a school system if they had been hearing.

In order to compare programs on achievement in the twelfth grade, we regressed ninth grade achievement and several demographic characteristics against twelfth grade achievement to create an expected twelfth grade achievement score. We then averaged the individual twelfth grade scores and the individual adjusted scores by program and plotted them against each other. What this gave us was a sense of which programs on the average had the higher or lower achievement than would have been expected based on the kids in ninth grade.

Our two "poorest" schools at opposite ends of the country fell above where we would have expected them to be.

While the two programs differed in many respects, one thing was common to both programs: a dedicated vocational training program. In both programs, there were dedicated and pro-active individuals who managed the vocational training programs. In one school, some of the deaf children would be the first members of their family to move off welfare because they could hold a paying job. In the other program, deaf youngsters might not hold the same types of jobs as their parents but they were on their own way to making salaries comparable to their parents.

By contrast, two programs that had very successful ninth grade students, who fell below their expected achievement levels in twelfth grade, did not have a clear vocational focus. Their deaf educational programs were like the general education programs: graduates went to college or didn't. If you wanted to go to college, the program worked well for you. If you didn't the program had few if any alternatives.

In our fear of holding children back from their "true potential" we have lost our direction. Not every deaf child will become president of Gallaudet anymore than every hearing child will or will want to become president of Harvard or Stanford or Yale. Some people will find a livelihood, satisfaction, and a life in working in service or manufacturing jobs. Out of fear of restricting a child, we must not force him or her into an all or nothing situation. Or worse, we let them drift without any direction because we will not offer them a goal.

Active Support for Social Development

As you read the last heading, you no doubt assumed that we meant that the individual who must make an effort is the deaf child. On the contrary, we meant that the program for the deaf must make an effort on behalf of the child. Just as we did with achievement, we also looked at program wide averages for the measures of socialization as part of our preliminary wade through the data. On the measure of orientation to hearing peers and orientation to deaf peers, we found two programs that were high on both measures. They shared some interesting characteristics including the extensive use of interpreters, presentation of deafness in a positive way, and access to deaf extra-curricular activities. Both programs provided travel arrangements and interpreters for deaf students who wished to participate in extra-curricular activities. In addition, the programs had junior NAD chapters and over the years had participated in joint activities with either deaf adult clubs or the state residential school. Finally both programs had signing choirs or some other form of deaf performance art which may or may not have included hearing students.

If the primary rationale for mainstreaming deaf students is to reduce overall schooling costs, then mainstreaming will be a failure on at least some of the parameters that can be used to measure its effectiveness. Because deafness represents a communication barrier, there will always be a cost involved in overcoming that barrier. Because, as we have seen repeatedly elsewhere in this book, adolescents will not necessarily associate with each other without some motivation to do so, efforts will have to be made to provide motivating access to each other.

In the programs where deaf students showed more social interaction, the programs had made a substantial and consistent effort to provide opportunities for connections. From our research findings and observations we offer the following general comments about these efforts at providing good social connections for deaf students. Good programs offered many opportunities for participation in extracurricular activities and provided the necessary transportation and communication support so that activities were accessible to deaf students. These programs tended to have large numbers of deaf students, but also employed extensive mainstreaming. Deaf students had good opportunities to develop signing skills, as well as proficiency in speech. Students with strong signing skills, but weak proficiency in speech, may tend to spend more time in special classes, and those with greater speech proficiency may be more frequently mainstreamed, with the exact extent of mainstreaming based on communication, academic, and social considerations. Even for students who are mainstreamed for most of their classes, the presence of a large number of deaf peers in the program and opportunities to interact with them through placement of groups of deaf peers in hearing classes, through extracurricular activities, and through other activities (such as getting together for lunch) allows the deaf students to maintain frequent, close contact with each other. For further discussion on facilitation of the social development of deaf students in the public school setting, we recommend Higgins's (1989) outstanding book on socially integrating deaf and hearing students.

CONCLUSION

Turning to more educationally manageable issues, it should be noted that some deaf children in these programs are participating in extracurriculars and that extracurricular participation does promote greater social maturity at graduation and probably contributes to a better grade point average because of a greater commitment to schooling as an activity.

School programs are doing something right in the placement process because the degree of mainstreaming a child receives is a consistent predictor of social maturity and school achievement. Further work needs to be done to consider this issue in detail, but it appears from these results that current school practices are in general placing students appropriately in the long run as they move them out of special classes. The system is not perfect, but it is functioning.

At the same time, these findings suggest that not enough is being done in the special classes to prepare students academically. Properly placed and adequately supported students should achieve at the levels their own ability and motivation and their family's support will carry them. However, the students in special classes continue to fall behind.

An intriguing outcome of this study has been the observation that orientation towards deaf or hearing peers are relatively independent of each other, but that both are related to appropriate communication skills and to social competence. The ability of a deaf adult to decide whether to participate in the deaf world, the hearing world, or both should be the goal of publically funded education. The ultimate decision is the responsibility of the deaf person, but the school's are accountable for the quality of the preparation that individual has in order to make that decision.

Schools cannot be held accountable for reclusive personalities; however, they are accountable for two phenomenon. For the child the school program decides to retain in a special class, the school program has the responsibility to provide that child access to the adult deaf community as well as to deaf peers in residential schools with whom they may share common interests. For the child who is encouraged into more mainstream situations, the schools have the responsibility to provide that child with communication support so that he or she is able to make the fullest use of that environment. Some of this occurred on a program by program basis.

Like the rest of American education from 1986 to 1991, some of the programs we looked at did wonderful jobs and others did not. They failed for many of the same reasons as the rest of American education struggled during this period of national neglect: inadequate funding for social programs and a national climate of violence and racism. They succeeded when adults treated children as human beings and when adults took their responsibilities toward the children seriously and purposively on a daily basis.

Local public school education for deaf children is here and will no doubt continue in some form into the future. Sometimes, it works miracles and sometimes it doesn't work at all. When the issue of the very existence of these kinds of programs is put aside, the problems of this system and the solutions to those problems become apparent. First, we saw children and teachers do better in programs where the political and governance integration of adult professionals was formalized. Second, regardless of the traits of the children, when goals were clearly defined and standards upheld, the children achieved higher than the average. Third, programs with "happy" individuals were programs where the students had more positive attitudes toward hearing peers and achieved at higher levels. Fourth, programs with more structured and supportive extracurricular opportunities produced graduates who were more interested in other people, regardless of their hearing status.

REFERENCES

Ainsworth, M. (1989). Attachments beyond infancy. *American Psychologist.* 44, 709–716.

Allen, T. & Osborn, T. (1984). Academic integration of hearing impaired students: Demographic, handicapping, and achievement factors. *American Annals of the Deaf,* 129, 100–113.

Allen, T., Rawlings, B., Schildroth, A. (1989). *Deaf Students and the School to Work Transition.* Baltimore: P.H. Brookes.

Alexander, K.L. & Entwistle, D.R. (1988). Achievement in the first two years of school: Patterns and processes. *Monographs of the Society for Research in Child Development.* 53, 2, 1–157.

Antia, S. (1982). Social Interaction of partially mainstreamed hearing impaired children. *American Annals of the Deaf.* 127, 18–25.

Antia, S. (1985). Social integration of hearing-impaired children: Fact or fiction? *Volta Review,* 87, 279–289.

Aronson, E., Blaney, N., Stephanson, C., Sikes, J., & Snapp, M. (1978). The jigsaw classroom. Beverly Hills, CA: Sage Publications.

Asher, S., Parkhurst, J., Hymel, S. & Williams, G. (1990). Peer rejection and loneliness in childhood. In S. Asher and J. Coie (Eds.) Peer rejection in childhood. (pp. 253–273.) New York: Cambridge University Press.

Barber, L. & McClellan, M. (1986). Looking at America's dropouts: Who are they? *Phi Delta Kappan.* 69, 264–267.

Beales, J.N. & Zemel, B. (1990). The effects of high school drama on social maturity. *School Counselor,* 38, 46–51.

Bodner-Johnson, B. (1986). The family environment and achievement of deaf students: A discriminant analysis. *Exceptional Children* 52, 5, 443–449.

Bond, K. & Beer, J. (1990). Dropping out and absenteeism in high school. *Psychological Reports.* 66, 817–818.

Bossert, S.T. (1979). *Tasks and social relationships in classrooms: A study of instructional organization and its consequences.* New York: Cambridge University Press.

Boyer, E.L. (1983). *High School.* New York: Harper & Row.

Cairns, R., Cairns, B. & Neckerman, H. (1989). Early school dropouts: Configurations and determinants. *Child Development.* 60, 1437–1452.

Caplan, N., Choy, M. & Whitmore, J. (1992). Indochinese refugee families and academic. *Scientific American.* 266, 2, 36–49.

Clements, B. (1990). What is a dropout? *Education Digest.* 56, 33–36.

Coleman, J.S. & Hoffer, T. (1987). *Public and Private High Schools.* New York: Basic Books, Inc.

Commission on Education of the Deaf (1988). Toward equality: Education of the deaf. Washington, DC: U.S. Government Printing Office.

Connell, J. (1990). Context, self, and action: A motivational analysis of self-system processes across the life-span. In D. Cicchetti (Ed.) *The Self in Transition: Infancy to Childhood.* Chicago, IL: University of Chicago Press.

Covington, M. & Beery, R. (1976). Self-Worth and School Learning. New York: Holt, Rinehart and Winston.

Davis, J. (1986). Academic placement in perspective. In D. Luterman (Ed.) Deafness in perspective. (pp. 205–224.) San Diego, CA: College Hill Press.

Durkin, D. (1975). A six year study of children who learned to read in school at the age of four. *Reading Research Quarterly.* 10, 1, 9–61.

Epstein, J.L. (1983). The influence of friends on achievement and affective outcomes. J.L. Epstein & N. Karweit (eds.) *Friends in School.* New York: Academic Press.

Epstein, J.L. (1983). Selection of friends in differently organized schools and classrooms. In J.L. Epstein & N. Karweit (eds.) *Friends in School.* New York: Academic Press.

Elser, R. (1959). The social position of hearing impaired children in the regular grades. *Exceptional Children.* 25, 305–309.

Farrugia, D. & Austin, G.F. (1980). A study of social-emotional adjustment patterns of hearing impaired students in different educational settings. *American Annals of the Deaf,* 125, 535–41.

Federal Register. (1977, August 23). Education of handicapped children, Implementation of Part B of the Education of the Handicapped Act, Part II. U.S. Department of Health, Education, and Welfare, Office of Education, Washington, DC.

Finn, C. (1989). Withdrawing from school. *Review of Educational Research.* 59, 2, 117–142.

Forehand, R., Long, N., Brody, G.H., & Fauber, R. (1986). Home predictors of young adolescents' school behavior and academic performance. *Child Development.* 57, 6, 1528–33.

Foster, S. (1988). Life in the mainstream: Reflections of deaf college freshmen on their experiences in the mainstreamed high school. *Journal of Rehabilitation of the Deaf,* 22, 37–56.

Foster, S. (1989). Social alienation and peer identification: A study of the social construction of deafness. *Human Organization,* 48, 226–235.

Furth, H. (1973). *Deafness and Learning: A Psychosocial Approach.* Belmont, CA: Wadsworth Publishing Co.

Gannon, J. (1981). *Deaf Heritage: A Narrative History of Deaf America.* Silver Spring, MD: National Association of the Deaf.

Garretson, M.D. (1977). The residential school. *Deaf American,* 29, 19–22.

Gaustad, M. & Kluwin, T. (1992). Patterns of Communication Among Deaf and Hearing Adolescents. In Kluwin, T.N., Moores, D.F., Gaustad, M.G. (eds.) *Toward Defining the Effective Public School Program for Deaf Students.* New York: Teachers College Press.

Glickman, N. (1986). Cultural identity, deafness, and mental health. *Journal of Rehabilitation of the Deaf,* 29, 1–10.

Gottman, J. & Mettetal, G. (1986). Speculations about social and affective development:

Friendship and acquaintanceship through adolescence. In J.M. Gottman & J.G. Parker *Conversations of friends: Speculations on Affective Development*, Cambridge: Cambridge University Press.

Greenberg, M.T. (1983). Stress and coping: A treatment model for deaf clients. Paper presented at the Northwest Association for Mental Health and Deafness, Seattle, WA.

Greenberg, M.T. & Kusche, C.A. (1989). Cognitive, personal, and social development of deaf children and adolescents. In M. Wang, M. Reynolds, & H. Walberg (Eds.) *Handbook of Special Education: Research and Practice.* (pp. 95-132). New York: Pergamon Press.

Greenberg, M.T., Kusche, C.A., Calderon, R., & Gustafson, R. The PATHS Curriculum (2nd Edition), Department of Psychology, University of Washington, 1983.

Griffen, S. (1988). Student activities in the middle school: What do they contribute? *NASSP Bulletin*, 72, 87-92.

Gutowski, T.W. (1988). Student initiative and the origins of the high school extracurriculum: Chicago, 1880-1915. *History of Education Quarterly*, 28, 49-72.

Hagborg, W. (1987). Hearing-Impaired Students and sociometric ratings: An exploratory study. Volta Review, 89, 4, 221-228.

Hansell, S. & Karweit, N. (1983). Curricular placement, friendship networks, and status attainment in J.L. Epstein & N. Karweit (eds.) *Friends in School.* New York: Academic Press.

Hatch, J.A. (1987). Peer interaction and the development of social competence. *Child Study Journal*, 17, 169-183.

Heller, M. (1987). The role of language in the formation of ethnic identity. In J. Phinney & M. Rotheram (Eds.), *Children's ethnic socialization: Pluralism and development* (pp. 180-200). Newbury Park, CA: Sage.

Holcomb, T.K. (1990). Deaf students in the mainstream: A study in social assimilation. Unpublished doctoral dissertation, University of Rochester, Rochester, NY.

Holland, A. & Andre, T. (1987). Participation in extracurricular activities in secondary school: What is known, what needs to be known? *Review of Educational Research*, 57, 437-466.

Hopper, M. & Stinson, M.S. (1987). Participation of deaf athletes in Rochester Institute of Technology varsity sports. National Technical Institute for the Deaf, Rochester, NY.

Ingersoll, G.M. (1989). *Adolescents.* Englewood Cliffs, NJ: Prentice-Hall.

Jacobs, L.M. (1989). *A Deaf Adult Speaks Out.* (3rd Ed.). Washington, DC: Gallaudet University Press.

Janesick, V. & Moores, D. (1992). Ethnic and Cultural Considerations in Kluwin, T.N., Moores, D.F., Gaustad, M.G. (eds.) *Toward Defining the Effective Public School Program for Deaf Students.* New York: Teachers College Press.

Johnson, D. (1980). Group processes: Influences of student-student interactions on school outcomes. In J. McMillan (Ed.) *The Social Psychology of School Learning.* (pp. 123-168.) New York: Academic Press.

Johnson, H. & Griffith, P. (1986). The instructional pattern of two fourth-grade spelling classes: A mainstream issue. *American Annals of the Deaf.* 131, 331-38.

Karweit, N. (1983). Extracurricular activities and friendship selection. In J.L. Epstein & N. Karweit (Eds.) Friends in school: Patterns of selection and influence in secondary schools (pp. 131–139). New York: Academic Press.

Karweit, N. & Hansell, S. (1983). School organization and friendship selection in J.L. Epstein & N. Karweit (eds.) *Friends in School.* New York: Academic Press.

Kaufman, M.J., Gottlieb, J., Agard, J.A. & Kukic, A. (1975). Mainstreaming: Toward an explication of the construct. *Focus on Exceptional Children,* 7, 1–13.

Keith, T. & Keith, V. (1992). Effects of Parental Involvement on eighth grade achievement: JSREL analysis of NELS-88 data. Paper presented at the annual meeting of the American Educational Research Association, San Francisco, CA.

King, S. (1992). The career development of young people with hearing impairments in Kluwin, T.N., Moores, D.F., Gaustad, M.M. (eds.) *Toward Defining the Effective Public School Program for Deaf Students.* New York: Teachers College Press.

Kinard, E.M. & Reinherz, H. (1987). School aptitude and achievement in children of adolescent mothers. *Journal of Youth and Adolescence,* 16, 1, 69–87.

Kirsh, B. (1983). The use of directives as indication of status among preschool children in J. Fine & R.O. Freedle (eds.) *Developmental Issues in Discourse Norwood, N.J.:* Ablex Publishing Corp.

Kirsh, C.E., Ham, M., & Richards, M.H. (1989). The sporting life: Athletic activities during early adolescence. *Journal of Youth and Adolescence,* 18–601–615.

Klima, E.S. & Bellugi, U. (1979). *The Signs of Language.* Cambridge, MA: Harvard University Press.

Kluwin, T.N. (in press). The cumulative effects of mainstreaming on the achievement of Deaf adolescents. *Exceptional Children.*

Kluwin, T.N. (1992a). What does "Local Public School" program mean? T.N. Kluwin. Public School Book.

Kluwin, T.N. (1992b). Considering the efficacy of mainstreaming from the classroom perspective. In Kluwin, T.N., Moores, D.F., Gaustad, M.G. (eds.) *Toward Defining the Effective Public School Program for Deaf Students.* New York: Teachers College Press.

Kluwin, T.N. (1991). Consumer motivated research to development: The rationale for the national research to development network. D.F. Moores & K.P. Meadow-Orlans (eds.) *Educational and Developmental* Aspects of Deafness. Washington, D.C.: Gallaudet University Press.

Kluwin, T.N. & Gaustad, G. (1992). How family factors influence school achievement in Kluwin, T.N., Moores, D.F., Gaustad, M.G. (eds.) *Toward Defining the Effective Public School Program for Deaf Students.* New York: Teachers College Press.

Kluwin, T.N., Blennerhasset, L., & Sweet, C. (1990). The revision of an instrument to measure the capacity of hearing impaired adolescents to cope. *Volta Review.* 1990, 92, 6, 283–292.

Kluwin, T.N. & Gaustad, M.G. (1991). Predicting family communication choices. *American Annals of the Deaf.* 1991, 136, 1, 28–34.

Kluwin, T.N. & Kelly, A.B. (1990). Application of a Process Oriented Writing Program for Hearing Impaired Students in Public Schools. Final Report for OSERS: Grant #023HH7003. Washington, D.C.: Gallaudet University, January.

Kluwin, T. & Moores, D. (1985). The effects of integration on the mathematics achievement of hearing impaired adolescents. *Exceptional Children.* 52, 2, 153–60.

Kluwin, T. & Moores, D. (1989). Mathematics achievement of hearing impaired adolescents in different placements. *Exceptional Children.* 55, 4, 327–35.

Kluwin, T.N. & Sweet, C. (1990, April). Coping strategies needed for social success by hearing-impaired students in local school programs. In A. O'Donnell (Chr.), The affective costs of mainstreaming for the hearing-impaired adolescent. Symposium conducted at the annual meeting of the American Educational Research Association, Boston, MA.

Kottke, J.L., Cowan, G. & Pfahler, D.J. (1988). Development of two scales of coping: an initial investigation. *Educational and Psychological Measurement.* 48, 737–742.

Ladd, G., Munson, H. & Miller, J. (1984). Social integration of deaf adolescents in secondary-level mainstreamed programs. *Exceptional Children,* 50, 420–428.

Lane, H. (1992). *The Mask of Benevolence.* New York: Alfred A. Knopf.

Larrivee, B. (1985). *Effective Teaching for Successful Mainstreaming.* New York: Longman.

Libbey, S.S. & Pronovost, W. (1980). Communication practices of mainstreamed hearing-impaired adolescents. *Volta Review.* 82, 4, 197–220.

Luterman, D. (1987). *Deafness in the Family.* Boston: College Hill Publications.

Meadow, K.P. (1980). *Deafness and Child Development.* Berkeley: University of California Press.

Meadow, K.P. (1983a). Revised manual. Meadow/Kendall Socio-Emotional Assessment Inventory for Hearing-Impaired Children. Washington, DC: Pre-College Programs, Gallaudet Research Institute.

Meadow, K.P. (1983b). An instrument for assessment of social-emotional adjustment in hearing-impaired preschoolers, *American Annals of the Deaf,* 128–826–834.

Mertens, D. (1989). Social experiences of hearing-impaired high school youth. *American Annals of the Deaf,* 134, 15–19.

Moores, D.F. (1992). The collision of reality and expectations. In T.N. Kluwin, D.F. Moores, & M.G. Gaustad (Eds.) *Toward Effective Public School Programs for Deaf Students* (pp. 238–242.) New York: Teacher's College Press.

Moores, D.F., Kluwin, T.N. & Mertens, D. (1985). *High School Programs for Deaf Students in Metropolitan Areas.* Gallaudet Research Institute Research Monograph No. 3, Washington, DC: Gallaudet University.

Musselman, C.R., Lindsay, P.H. & Wilson, A.K. (1988). Am evaluation of recent trends in preschool programming for hearing-impaired children. *Journal of Speech and Hearing Disorders,* 53, 71–88.

Newman, P.R. (1979). Persons and settings: A comparative analysis of the quality and range of social interaction in two high schools. In J.G. Kelly (ed.) *Adolescent Boys in High School: A Psychological Study of Coping and Adaptation.* Hillsdale, NJ: Lawrence Erlbaum Assoc.

Page, E.B. & Keith, T.Z. (1981). Effects of U.S. private schools: A technical analysis of two recent claims. *Educational Researcher.* 10, 7, 7–17.

Patterson, J.M. & McCubbin, H.I. (1987). ACOPE, adolescent-coping orientation for problem experiences. In H.I. McCubbin & A. Thompson (eds.) Family assessment interventions for research and practice. Madison: University of Wisconsin Press.

Putallaz, M. & Heflin, A.H. (1986). Toward a model of peer acceptance. In J.M. Gottman & J.G. Parker *Conversations of friends: Speculations on Affective Development Cambridge:* Cambridge University Press.

Quarrington, B. & Solomon, B. (1975). A current study of the social maturity of deaf students. *Canadian Journal of Behavioral Science,* 7, 70–77.

Raimondo, D., & Maxwell, M. (1987). The modes of communication used in junior and senior high school classrooms by hearing-impaired students and their teachers and peers. *Volta Review.* 89, 6, 263–275.

Rittenhouse, R.K., Ruhn, C.H. & Moreau, L.E. (1989). Educational interpreter services for hearing impaired students: Provider and consumer disagreements. Journal of the American Deafness and Rehabilitation Association, 22 (3), 57–62.

Rumberger, R.W. (1987). High school dropouts: A review of issues and evidence. *Review of Educational Research.* 57, 101–121.

Saur, R., Lane, C., Hurley, B. & Opton, K. (1986). Dimensions of mainstreaming. *American Annals of the Deaf,* 131, 325–330.

Saur, R., Popp-Stone, M. & Hurley-Lawrence, E. (1987). The classroom participation of mainstreamed hearing-impaired college students. *Volta Review.* 89, 6, 277–287.

Sebald, H. (1989). Adolescents' peer orientation: Changes in the support system during the past three decades. *Adolescence,* 24, 96, 937–946.

Seginer, R. (1983). Parents' educational expectations and children's academic achievements: A literature review. *Merrill-Palmer Quarterly,* 29, 1, 1–23.

Schildroth, A. (1988). Recent changes in the educational placement of deaf students. *American Annals of the Deaf,* 61–67.

Schlesinger, H.S. & Meadow, K.P. (1972). *Sound and Sign: Childhood Deafness and Mental Health.* Berkeley: University of California Press.

Schloss, P.S. & Smith, M.A. (1990). *Teaching Social Skills to Hearing-Impaired Students.* Washington, DC: Alexander Graham Bell Association for the Deaf.

Schulz, M., Toles, R., Rice, W., Brauer, I., Harvey, I. (1986). The association of dropout rates with student attributes. Paper presented at the annual meeting of the American Educational Research Association, San Francisco, CA.

Sims, D., Walter, G. & Whitehead, R. (1982). (Eds.) *Deafness and Communication: Assessment and Training.* Baltimore, MD: Williams and Wilkins.

Skinner, E.A., Wellborn, J.G. & Connell, J.P. (1990). What it takes to do well in school and whether I've got it: A process model of perceived control and children's engagement and achievement in school. *Journal of Educational Psychology,* 82, 22–32.

Stewart, D.A. & Stinson, M.S. (1992). The role of sport and extracurricular activities in shaping socialization patterns. In T.N. Kluwin, D.F. Moores, & M.G. Gaustad (Eds.) *Toward Effective Public School Programs for Deaf Students.* (pp. 129–148.) New York: Teacher's College Press.

Stinson, M.S. (in press). Affective and social development. In R. Nowell and L. Marshak (Eds.), *Understanding Deafness and the Rehabilitative Process.* Needham Heights, MA: Allyn and Bacon.

Stinson, M.S., Chase, K.W. & Kluwin, T.N. (1990, April). Self-perceptions of social relationships in hearing-impaired adolescents. Paper presented at the annual meeting of the American Educational Research Association, Boston.

Stinson, M.S., Siple, L.A., Chase, K.W. & Bondi-Wolcott, J. (1990, October). Perceptions of social relationships by hearing-impaired adolescents enrolled in day classes and residential schools. Paper presented at the National Conference on the Habilitation and Rehabilitation of Hearing-Impaired Adolescents, Omaha, NE.

Stinson, M.S. & Whitmire, K. (1990). Factors influencing self-perceptions of social relationships among hearing-impaired adolescents in England. Unpublished data, National Technical Institute for the Deaf, Rochester, NY.

Stinson, M.S. & Whitmire, K. (1991). Self-perceptions of social relationships among hearing-impaired adolescents in England. *Journal of the British Association of Teachers of the Deaf,* 15, 104–114.

Stinson, M.S. & Whitmire, K. (1992). Students' views of their social relationships. In T. Kluwin, M. Gaustad, & D. Moores (Eds.), *Toward Effective Public School Programs for Deaf Students.* New York: Teacher's College Press.

Svec, H. (1986). Overestimation of academic competence by high school dropouts. Psychological Reports. 59, 669–670.

Tedesco, L.A. & Gaier, E.L. (1988). Friendship bonds in adolescence. *Adolescence.* 23, 127–136.

Walberg, H. (1984). Improving the productivity of American Schools. *Educational Leadership.* 41, (8), 19–27.

Wentzel, K.R. (1991). Social competence at school: Relation between social responsibility and academic achievement. *Review of Educational Research,* 61, 1–24.

Wilks, J. (1986). The relative importance of parents and friends in adolescent decision making. *Journal of Youth and Adolescence.* 15, 323–334.

Wolk, S., Karchmer, M.A., Schildroth, A. (1982). Patterns of academic and non-academic integration among hearing impaired students in special education. Gallaudet Research Institute, Series R. No. 9., Washington, DC: Gallaudet University.

Woodward, J. & Allen, T. (18987). Classroom use of ASL by teachers. *Sign Language Studies,* 54, (1), 1–10.

Wrubel, J., Benner, P. & Lazarus, R.S. (1981). Social competence from the perspective of stress and coping. In J. Wine & M. Smye (Eds.), *Social Competence* (pp. 61–99). New York: Guilford.

Zeitlin, S., Williamson, G.G. & Rosenblatt, W.P. (1987). The coping with stress model: Counseling approach for families with a handicapped child. *Journal of Counseling and Development.* 65, 443–446.

INDEX

A

Achievement, 29, 47, 123, 127–129
    dropouts and, 69–71
    family and, 48
    mainstreaming and, 55–56, 144
    social maturity and, 112
    ACOPE, 23–24
Adolescents, 23
Affiliation traits, 75, 76
    preferred associates, 77, 79, 81
    status system, 74, 76
    trait visibility and, 74, 76
Ainsworth, M., 115
Allen, T., 16, 48, 59, 66, 1124
Alexander, K., 33
Annual Survey of Hearing Impaired Children and Youth (Gallaudet University), 19
Antia, S., 3, 114
Aronson, E.
Asher, S., 1122
Asians, 38

B

Baby boom, 4
Beales, J., 90
Blacks, 6–7, 49–50, 55
    speech skill and, 49
Bond, K., 66
Bossert, S., 74
Boyer, E., 5, 57, 58, 66

C

Carins, N., 66
Centralized programs, 11–12
Clements, B., 66

Coleman, J., 15, 57, 58, 60
Communication mode, 27–28, 77
    impact of, 144
    in local public school programs, 84–85
    peer interaction and, 78, 84–85
    in socialization process, 78
    social relationships and, 77, 80–81, 101
    skills, 30
Course selection, 53ff
    placement and, 57–66
    reports, 20

D

Davis, J., 111, 120
Deaf culture, 92, 93, 106
    deaf peers, 125, 137–138
    orientation to, 114–118, 151
Drop-outs, 66–71

E

Elementary school experiences, 28, 42–44, 48
English, 58–59, 60, 64–65
Enrollment
    history, 20
Ethnicity, 84, 106
Extracurricular activities, 15, 81
    achievement and, 90
    attitudes of coaches, 93
    degree of participation, 97–105
    social outcomes, 90–91, 92–93
    structured activities, 91
    type of participation, 98–101, 105–106
    transportation and, 81–82, 93, 102–103

F

FACES, 26–27

Family, 147
   characteristics of, 28, 33
   communication practices, 39–40
   education, 35–37
   environment, 26–27, 33
   income and, 35
   marital status, 38–39
   parental expectations, 40–42, 145
   resources of, 101, 128, 130, 143
   social class and, 26, 34, 37
Farrago, D., 73
Finn, C., 66
Forehand, R., 33
Foster, S., 73, 76, 114, 115, 122
Firth, H., 110

G

Gallaudet University, 17
Garretson, M., 87, 88, 107
Gaustad, M., 73, 76, 78, 79, 121, 126
Gender traits, 55, 69, 101–103, 105–106,
   119–120, 128, 130, 131, 143, 148
Glickman, N., 116, 121
Gottman, J., 73
Grade point average, 123, 129
Griffen, S., 89
Gutowski, T., 87

H

Hagborg, W., 75, 77
Hansell, S., 74
Hatch, J., 75, 109, 110
Hearing loss, 117, 118, 119, 143
Hearing peers, 139
   orientation to, 114–116, 118–121, 151
Heller, M., 117
Hispanics, 6–7, 44, 55
Holcomb, T., 91, 94, 95, 104
Holland, A., 87, 90, 91, 106

I

Instrumentation, 19–25
Integration, See Mainstreaming.
Interaction skills, 74–76
Ingersoll, G., 74
Interpreters, 125, 136

Invariable traits, 15, 19, 28, 85, 123–124, 136

J

Jacobs, L., 88
Janesick, V., 106
Johnson, D., 109, 122
Johnson, H., 124
Junior National Association of the Deaf, 10, 84

K

Karweit, N., 74, 75, 88, 89, 91
Kaufman, M., 114
Keith, T., 127
King, S., 59
Kluwin, T., 8, 12, 17, 19, 33, 34, 47, 48, 53, 110, 114, 124, 127, 146, 147

L

Ladd, G., 74, 110
Lane, H., 87, 109
Larrivee, B., 125
Longitudinal study, 5–6
Libbey, S., 73, 76, 78, 126

M

Mainstreaming, 54–66, 80–81, 113, 145
Mathematics, 60–62, 134–135, 140
Meadow, K., 110, 114
Meadow-Kendall Social Emotional Inventory, 22–23, 110
Mertens, D., 122
Moores, D., 3, 5, 94

N

National Technical Institution for the Deaf (NTID), 95
Ninth grade, 46–51, 56, 59, 131–132

O

Operational Definitions, 28–32
Outcomes, 17

Index

P

Page, E., 33
Patterson, J.
PL 94-142, 3, 4
Peer Interaction, 72ff, 125–126
Placement, 3, 55–56, 128, 133, 144
    Peers and, 119–120
    Social maturity and, 112, 113
    Traits of students and, 124
Preschool, 42
Program types, 8–15
Putallaz, M., 75

Q

Quarrington, B., 111

R

Race, 35, 133, 143, 145–146
Raimondo, D., 73, 76, 78, 126
Reading comprehension, 132, 134
Research design, 17–19

S

Saur, R., 73, 126
Sebald, H., 74
Seginer, R., 34, 42
Schlesinger, H., 111
School Activity Structures, 73
Schloss, P., 121
School Efforts, 14–16
Schulz, M., 66
Science,
    courses taken, 63–64
Sign language, 50, 79–82, 84, 133
Signing skill, 117
Sims, D., 120
Skinner, E., 111
Social Activity, Scale, 24–26
Social competence, 30, 48, 86, 109–122
    social relationships and, 80, 84, 86
Social maturity, 110–114, 128, 130
Socialization process,
    extracurricular activities and, 89, 94–96
Social relationships, 82, 114, 125

Sign skill and, 80–81, 116–117
Speech skill and, 80–81
Social Studies,
    courses taken, 60, 62–63
Special class placement, 55–57, 65
    achievement and, 55
    characteristics of students in, 57
    See also Mainstreaming,
Speech, 49–50, 81, 128–129, 130
Sports,
    participation in, 98–100
    See also extra-curricular activities
Stanford Achievement Test Hearing Impaired
    Version (SAT–HI), 19, 69
Stewart, D., 76, 87, 88, 91, 92, 94, 97, 104, 106
Stinson, M., 76, 91, 109, 110, 114, 115, 116, 117,
    120, 121, 122, 126
Suburban programs, 9, 55
Sec, H., 66

T

Tedesco, L., 75
Telecommunications Devices for the Deaf
    (TDD), 6
Tracking, 57–59
Transportation, 81–82
    See also Extracurricular participation

U

Urban Schools, 10–11

V

Value systems,
    adolescent, 74
Vocational education, 61–62

W

Walberg, H., 123, 126
Wentzel, K., 111, 121
Wilks, J., 75
Wolk, S., 124
Woodward, J., 78
Writing evaluation, 20–22, 134
Wrubel, J., 109